D1304855

Secret
SAUCE

HOW TO
PACK YOUR MESSAGES WITH
PERSUASIVE PUNCH

❧ HARRY MILLS ❧

AMACOM

AMERICAN MANAGEMENT ASSOCIATION

New York • Atlanta • Brussels • Chicago • Mexico City • San Francisco
Shanghai • Tokyo • Toronto • Washington, DC

American Management Association: www.amanet.org

This publication is designed to provide accurate and authoritative information in regard to the subject matter covered. It is sold with the understanding that the publisher is not engaged in rendering legal, accounting, or other professional service. If legal advice or other expert assistance is required, the services of a competent professional person should be sought.

Library of Congress Cataloging-in-Publication Data
Names: Mills, Harry, 1950- author.
Title: Secret sauce : how to pack your messages with persuasive punch /
    by Harry Mills.
Description: New York, NY : AMACOM, [2017] | Includes bibliographical references.
Identifiers: LCCN 2016042355 (print) | LCCN 2016056856 (ebook) | ISBN
    9780814438060 (hardcover) | ISBN 9780814438077 (eBook)
Subjects: LCSH: Persuasion (Psychology) | Interpersonal communication. |
    Business communication.
Classification: LCC BF637.P4 M523 2017 (print) | LCC BF637.P4 (ebook) | DDC
    153.8/52--dc23
LC record available at https://lccn.loc.gov/2016042355

10 9 8 7 6 5 4 3 2 1

To Mary Anne
My Secret Sauce

CONTENTS

PART II: Lessons from the Frontline

Part I

The
New Alchemy
of Message
Making

" **The secret to successful persuasion is knowing how to dissolve and eliminate resistance."**

—Harry Mills

1.

Secret Sauce

The Magic Recipe for Measuring Persuasive Impact

Our message-making needs reinvention

When it comes to messages, what worked in the past won't work today. Two decades of destabilizing and accelerating change have profoundly changed the psychology of how, when and why customers respond to persuasive messages.

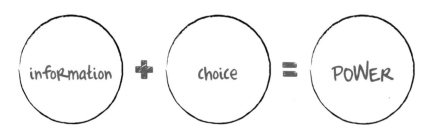

For the first time in history the customer holds the trump cards

Digital-driven technologies have armed buyers with anytime, anywhere access to the choices and information they need to call the shots.

Once customers gain power, they become increasingly skeptical, pay less attention and become less reverential to those who try to influence and sell to them.

Marketers and brands are becoming less influential

In our Google-driven world the influence brands, marketers and salespeople have over customer decisions is rapidly diminishing.

Trust in business is at an all-time low. Customers increasingly base their decisions on reviews from other users, web accessed expert opinions, and price comparison apps.

Stanford professor Itamar Simonson and best-selling author Emanuel Rosen in their book *Absolute Value: What Really Influences Customers in the Age of (Nearly) Perfect Information* write that customers are influenced by two sources of information which they label **M** and **O**.

M is shorthand for the information buyers get from marketing information sources. **O** is shorthand for the information buyers get from other sources. In a Google-driven world buyers' decisions are being increasingly influenced by **O**.[1]

Customers increase their use of **O** when:

1. A buying decision is important.
2. A buying decision involves increased risk and uncertainty.

Why? Because customers inherently trust **O** sources more than **M** sources.[2]

M AND O POWER SHIFT

Information from marketers
Branding
Advertising
Product/service information

Information from other sources
Influential friends and colleagues
Reviews from end users, consumers
Third-party reports
Expert advisers

Are digital communication technologies rewiring our brains?

We live in a world where a phone originally invented as a talking device has become a "weapon of personal empowerment."

In her book *Decoding the New Consumer Mind*, Kit Yarrow says the pervasiveness of digital technology has transformed our lives.[3]

In the new digital world she reports:

► We skim and scan rather than read.
► We're bombarded and interrupted by a relentless barrage of information.
► We're conditioned to want everything faster.
► We are increasingly addicted to stimulation and speed.
► We're becoming less and less tolerant of anything that requires patience.[4]

In his book *iBrain: Surviving the Technological Alteration of the Modern Mind*, Gary Small describes the new mental state we live in as "continuous partial attention."[5]

We are drowning in a tsunami of information. Consulting company Excelacom reports 150 million emails are sent every minute across the Internet. In comparison, the U.S.

Postal Service processes just 353,000 pieces of mail each minute—that's about 0.2 percent the number of emails sent. And that's not all. In the span of just one minute:

- ► 347,000 tweets are tweeted.
- ► 20.8 million messages are sent on WhatsApp.
- ► 527,760 photos are shared.[6]

The firehose

Shlomo Bernartzi, a professor at UCLA's Anderson School of Management and author with Jonah Lehrer of *The Smarter Screen* uses the metaphor of a firehose to describe the deluge of data that characterizes our information age.

He tells us in ancient times the flow of data and messages that competed for our attention was more "like the drip of water from a leaky faucet." By the middle of the 20th century the flow of information was more like a steady flow of water coming out of a kitchen faucet.

Since the 1980s computers have been increasing the quantity of information exponentially. The magnitude of data is now so great it is as if our kitchen faucet has been replaced by a high pressure firehose which sprays us in the face with a deluge of data.

A firehose unleashes 125 times more gallons per minute than a kitchen faucet. But we can't drink it, because the mouth has fixed constraints. It doesn't matter how much water flows by our face—we will never be able to gulp more than a few sips at a time.

When it comes to how much information our brains can process, the limiting factor is rarely what's on the screen. The amount of information will almost always exceed the capacity of our mind to take it in. Instead we are limited by a scarcity of attention; by our inability to focus on more than a few things at the same time.[7] This problem is compounded by our brain's fundamental limitations and constraints.

According to psychological lore, when it comes to items of information the mind can cope with before confusion sets in, the "magic number" is seven.

In 1956, American psychologist George Miller published a paper in the influential journal *Psychological Review* arguing that the mind could cope with a maximum of only seven chunks of information. The paper "The Magical Number Seven, Plus or Minus Two, Some Limits on Our Capacity for Processing Information" has since become one of the most highly cited articles and has been judged by the *Psychological Review* as its most influential paper of all time.

But UNSW professor of psychiatry Gordon Parker says a re-analysis of the experiments used by Miller shows he missed the correct number by a wide mark. Professor Parker says a closer look at the evidence shows the human mind copes with a maximum of four "chunks" of information. Not seven.

To remember a seven numeral phone number, say 6458937, we need to break it into four chunks: 64. 58. 93. 7. Basically four is the limit to our perception.

"Our brain filters billions of pieces of information streaming into our senses into a maximum of three or four conscious items." Experiments show we can easily keep track of three items relatively easily. We can competently handle four items—though our accuracy diminishes. Most find handling five items virtually impossible.[8]

"Surprisingly, our working memory limit of a handful of items is basically the same as a monkey's brain, even though a monkey's brain is about one fifteenth the size of ours."[9]

Whenever the volume of information pounding our brains exceeds its ability to process it, we become overwhelmed. The result: bad decisions.

One way of coping is to take shortcuts.

A new study by scientists at Columbia University and the French National Institute shows 59 percent of links shared on social media *have never actually been clicked.* In other words, most people appear to retweet news without ever reading it.[10]

The evidence suggests people are more willing to share an article than read it. The study co-author Arnaud Legout says "this is typical of modern information consumption. People form an opinion based on a summary or a summary of summaries, without making the effort to go deeper."

The Sauce Persuasion Test

For a message to pack a persuasive punch in our information-saturated, screen-dominated world, it must pass the SAUCE test.

Persuasive messages must be:

S imple: One central truth, easy to grasp and picture

A ppealing: Different, valuable, and personalized

U nexpected: Surprising, intriguing, and seductive

C redible: Trusted, transparent, and verifiable

E motional: Warm, arousing, and plot-driven

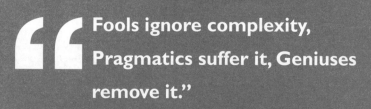

**Fools ignore complexity,
Pragmatics suffer it, Geniuses
remove it."**

—Alan Peritis

2.

Simple

**One Central Truth,
Easy to Grasp and Picture**

The Pope asked Michelangelo: "Tell me the secret to your genius. How have you created the statue of David, the masterpiece of all masterpieces?" Michelangelo answered: "It's simple. I removed everything that is not David."[11]

Complex is easy. Simple is hard.

Here is the first version of a speech sometimes hailed by theater lovers as the greatest speech in any play ever written.

> "To be, or not to be, aye there's the point,
> To die, to sleep, is that all? Aye all:
> No, to sleep, to dream, aye marry there it goes,"

Here is the final version:

"To be, or not to be, that is the question—
Whether 'tis Nobler in the mind to suffer
The Slings and Arrows of outrageous Fortune,
Or to take Arms against a Sea of troubles,"

Today, it's hard to imagine that the first version was even written by Shakespeare. The original draft comes from an early edition of the play which scholars call "The First Quarto."[12]

> Simple messages
> contain one central truth,
> are easy to grasp
> and picture.

THE THREE SIMPLE CRITERIA

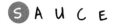

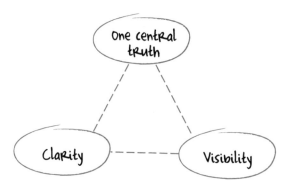

Simple messages contain one central truth

Success in messaging starts with determining the central truth of the one idea you most want to get across.

Ideas that pack a persuasive punch work much like proverbs. Proverbs, write Chip and Dan Heath, the authors of *Made to Stick,* represent the ideal of what is possible when you strip an idea down to a central truth "that is both simple and profound."[13]

The proverb "a bird in the hand is worth two in the bush" for example, has endured for over 2,500 years. The core idea warns us not to gamble a sure thing on something that's highly risky.

As it has spread across cultures the words have been adapted to fit local circumstances. The Swedes say "Rather one bird in the hand than ten in the woods". The Poles, "A sparrow in your hand is better than a pigeon on the roof". The Russians, "Better a titmouse in the hand than a crane in the sky". [14]

For a central truth to stick and gain traction it must:

- *Be distinctive and memorable.* We remember words that jolt and sparkle.
- *Ring true.* Words that exaggerate, over-promise or sound like typical corporate bull, do not attract: they repel. Customers switch off when companies use "fifty cent words to make a five cent point." [15]

Taglines

Brand taglines represent the perfect opportunity for companies to communicate their central truth simply and profoundly.

Take Microsoft's tagline "Your potential. Our passion." These words smell and sound corporate. They simply don't ring true. According to Steven Cone, author of *Powerlines:*

Words That Sell Brands, Grip Fans and Sometimes Change History, "It is hard to believe that a company with zillions of customers cares about me and my potential."[16]

Take the University of Chicago's School of Business MBA program tagline "Triumph in your moment of truth." What does this tagline mean? It doesn't make sense. It is another example of smart people using dumb words.[17]

Compare these ineffective taglines with two of the best.

De Beers' "A Diamond Is Forever" was penned in 1948 by copywriter Francis Gerety. It still resonates today. "Is there a better way," writes Steve Cone, "to say I love you? A better way to remind men and women what the gift of a diamond conveys?" Gerety's tagline transformed the diamond into a symbol of eternal love.[18]

In 2004 the Las Vegas Convention and Visitors Authority reacting to the downturn in tourists launched a "sexy and suggestive" tagline: *What Happens Here, Stays Here.* Previously, Las Vegas had been positioned as a great family destination, similar to Disneyland. But that positioning didn't ring true. Las Vegas is primarily for adults who come to escape from family pressures and live on the edge. The new positioning worked. The new tagline resonated and tourists returned.[19]

Simple messages are easy to grasp

Easy to grasp messages are clear and concise.

Clarity

In the digital world where we skim and scan rather than read, crystal-clear communications are a must. Long-winded, obscure phrases are message killers.

37signals (now called Basecamp) was founded in 1999 as a web design firm. In 2004 it became a software company with the release of Basecamp, an easy to use project management tool. Over 15 million people currently have Basecamp accounts.

Few companies enjoy a better reputation for communicating with crystal-clear clarity than Basecamp.

Here is a sampling of the crystal-clear messages they have used:

"We build software that does what you need and nothing you don't."

"Software should be easy. Our products are intuitive; you'll pick them up in seconds or minutes, not hours, days or weeks. We don't sell you training software because you don't need it."

"Long-term contracts are obscene. No one likes being locked into something they don't need anymore. Our customers can cancel at any time, no questions asked. No set up/termination fees, either."[20]

Conciseness

Time-starved readers are deterred by long, densely written communications. If you want to be noticed, remembered and passed along, make brevity your friend.

Short formats of everything are becoming much more popular. Many YouTube videos are now only 30 seconds long. The popular Ignite Talks allow speakers just five minutes each to speak on a topic. Ignite's slogan is "Enlighten us. But make it quick."[21]

Most salespeople have heard of the elevator pitch. It's a pitch that is brief enough to be delivered during an elevator ride. Recently, entrepreneurs are being urged to come up with an "escalator pitch". An escalator pitch is "a pitch short enough to make when you are on the up escalator, and your funding prospect is on the down escalator passing by."[22]

The idea took root in 2008, after Steve Boyd asked for "twitpitches" to help him determine which companies he would meet at the Web 2.0 Expo in San Francisco. Because a twitpitch is sent via Twitter it cannot be longer than 140 characters, the maximum length of a tweet.[23]

In Hollywood novelists and screenwriters use one sentence, "high concept" pitches to capture the attention of agents or investors. The movie *Alien* was successfully pitched as "*JAWS* in space".[24]

However, never forget there is a tradeoff between clarity and brevity. Clarity in the end is about finding the right level of detail for the circumstances.

Simple, persuasive messages can be pictured

Social psychologists Anthony Pratkanis and Elliot Aronson were asked by a local power company to help sell the advantages of home insulation. The utility offered householders a free energy audit. A trained auditor would go through each consumer's house identifying the requirements to make it more energy efficient. The utility even provided an interest-free loan.

The benefits seemed obvious. Energy savings of 40 percent were common and power savings following the installation of insulation would quickly pay for the cost of the loan.

The puzzle was while large numbers of home owners requested a home audit, only 15 percent of them actually followed the advice of the auditor—even though clearly it made excellent financial sense.

Why? Researchers interviewed several home owners and discovered that most had a hard time believing that small cracks under a door or the lack of insulation in an attic could result in such a large energy loss.

To solve this problem, Pratkanis and Aronson trained the auditors to communicate their findings and recommendations with words that could be pictured. They advised the auditors to tell this to the homeowners:

> "Look at all the cracks around that door! It may not seem much to you but if you were to add up all the cracks around each of these doors, you'd have the equivalent of a hole the circumference of a basketball. Suppose someone poked a hole the size of a basketball in your living room wall. Think for a moment about all the heat that you would be losing from a hole that size—you'd want to patch that hole in your wall, wouldn't you? That's what weather-stripping does. And your attic totally lacks insulation. We professionals call that a 'naked attic'. It's as if your home is facing winter not just without an overcoat, but without any clothing at all! You wouldn't let your young kids run outside in the winter time without clothes on, would you? It's the same with your attic."

When homeowners heard this speech they signed up in droves. Where previously only 15 percent of the householders signed up, now 61 percent signed up to have their houses insulated. Vivid, picturable language had turned barely visible cracks into holes the size of basketballs. The idea of running around naked in winter also grabs attention and strongly encourages you to take action.[25]

Image-based metaphors

When professional persuaders want to describe abstract ideas, emotions and concepts, they search for an image-based metaphor.

James Geary, the author of *I Is an Other: The Secret Life of Metaphor and How It Shapes the Way We See Our World* writes "A metaphor is the process of giving a thing a name that belongs to something else. In *Romeo and Juliet* Shakespeare tells us "Juliet is the sun." Here Shakespeare gives the thing (Juliet) a name that belongs to something else (the sun)."

Geary continues, "On the surface, Juliet is nothing like the sun. Nevertheless she shines. Romeo is increasingly drawn by her gravitational pull. She is the center of the universe. She radiates heat. And her brightness can, of course, burn."

Shakespeare's metaphor tells us everything we need to know "about Juliet—and Romeo's feelings for her—in just four simple words." Is it any wonder Aristotle regarded metaphorical thinking as "a sign of genius."[26]

Metaphor is much more popular than we think. Researchers have discovered we use a metaphor every ten to twenty-five words. That adds up to about six metaphors a minute.[27]

Politicians know the power of metaphor. Abraham Lincoln's 1864 election campaign during the Civil War, *Don't Swap Horses In Midstream*, warned voters against making a change when times are uncertain. George W. Bush paraphrased the slogan in his 2004 reelection campaign with *Don't Change Horses Midstream*.[28]

Metaphors abound in advertising. Advertisers are in many ways professional metaphor makers.[29]

Here are a few of the more memorable ones:

- ☛ **Tropicana uses "Your daily ray of sunshine" to promote its orange juice.**
- ☛ **Taco Bell tells us to "Think outside the bun."**
- ☛ **AT&T told us to "Reach out and touch someone."**
- ☛ **Nissan says "Life is a journey, enjoy the ride."[30]**

> **Metaphors enhance the credibility of low credibility messages**
>
> ► Novel metaphors are more persuasive than familiar ones.
> ► Single, extended, novel metaphors introduced early in a message are especially persuasive.[31]

Pictures and graphics

In the world of skim and scan, consumers are favoring photos, visual cues and symbolism over words. The popularity of the infographic has exploded. Successful persuaders have responded by dramatically boosting the number of pictures and graphics they use.

The invention of the camera phone has amplified our love and addiction to visuals. The first camera phone appeared in 2002. Just ten years later Facebook users were uploading 300 million photos a day.

Facebook posts that have photos, for example, generate 53 percent more "likes" and 103 percent more comments than text-only posts.[32]

IS YOUR MESSAGE SIMPLE?

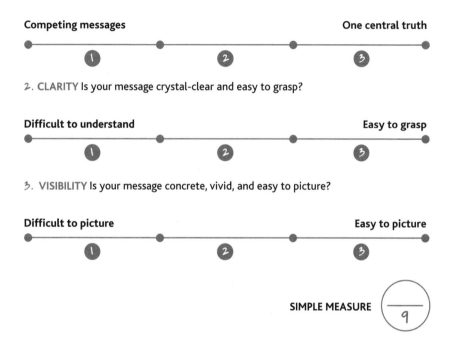

1. ONE CENTRAL TRUTH Has your message been stripped down to one central truth?

Competing messages   **One central truth**

    1   2   3

2. CLARITY Is your message crystal-clear and easy to grasp?

Difficult to understand   **Easy to grasp**

    1   2   3

3. VISIBILITY Is your message concrete, vivid, and easy to picture?

Difficult to picture   **Easy to picture**

    1   2   3

SIMPLE MEASURE $\dfrac{\quad}{9}$

"The punters know that the horse named Morality rarely gets past the post, whereas the nag named Self-Interest always runs a good race."

—Gough Whitlam,
former Australian prime minister

3.

Appealing

Different, Valuable, and Personalized

n the early 1990s, 31-year-old Alex Bogusky, then the creative director of a small ad agency, wrote what is today called the hitchhiker ad. It was designed as a press advert and displayed two images side-by-side.

The first image showed a man hitchhiking by the side of the road holding a cardboard sign with the name of a U.S. city written on it in black pen. "It could have been any hitchhiker, on any road, on any day." Above it was one bold-type word, "Sales".

The second image was similar; a man was hitchhiking by the side of a road holding a cardboard sign. But written on his sign in black ink was the line "Mom's for Thanksgiving". Above it was one bold-type word, "Marketing".

Bogusky, who today is referred to as the Elvis of advertising, wanted to show that the difference between sales and marketing was a persuasive message and to show that the agency that wrote the ad knew how to write messages that were compelling and appealing.[33]

Appealing messages are different

On January 9, 2007, Steve Jobs announced the launch of the iPhone, a device that would transform what a mobile phone could offer. While smartphone manufacturers kept adding more and more buttons and features, Apple went for minimalism. He offered a phone that was more capable than its competitors with less clutter.

> Appealing messages are
> different, valuable
> and appeal to self-interest

Here is Jobs' introduction to the first iPhone:

"The most advanced phones are called smartphones. They typically combine a phone, email, and a baby Internet. The problem is they are not so smart and they are not so easy to use.

Regular cell phones are definitely a little smarter, but they're actually harder to use. They're really complicated. Just for the basic stuff, people have a hard time figuring out how to use them.

What we want to do is make a leapfrog product that is way smarter than any mobile device has been and super easy to use. This is what iPhone is."[34]

THE THREE APPEALING CRITERIA

S (A) U C E

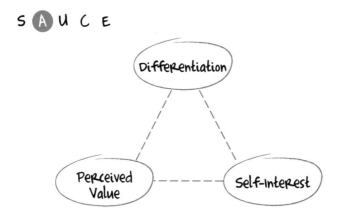

Appealing messages offer high perceived value

Think back to the late 1990s when MP3 players were struggling to win sales. The MP3 manufacturers pushed their tech and specs without much success. But as savvy marketer Bernadette Jiwa says, "People can't fall in love with 32MB and user interfaces."

Then along came Apple and the iPod with the sales message, "1000 songs in your pocket." Now that's persuasive.[36]

Virtually every iPod review repeated the iPod's "1000 songs in your pocket" message. Because the statement was so concise and compelling reviewers rarely edited or rephrased it. Talk about free advertising.

Appealing messages target self-interest

Dr. Kevin Dutton, an expert on the science of social influence and author of *Flipnosis: The Art of Split Second Persuasion* declares, "If you want the secret of persuasion in just a few simple words, it's easy. Appeal to the other party's self-interest—what they think is to their advantage."[37]

Compare the appeal of the promotion "apples contain vitamins and natural sugar" with "an apple a day keeps the doctor away." The first promotion describes facts or features about the apple; the second promotion describes how the apple will help the buyer. The second promotion sells the benefits of what the apple can do.

Features are cold, remote and impersonal; benefits are warm and tempting.

No one has understood this better than John Caples, one of the greatest copywriters of all time.

Caples is the man that penned what has been called "history's most famous ad." In 1925 Caples was asked to write an ad selling a home study course offered by the U.S. School of Music. The copy ran for four pages but it was the headline that engaged readers.

"They laughed when I sat down at the piano.
But when I started to play!"

Overnight it became a success. Comedians lampooned but other copywriters "borrowed from it, copied it, and paraphrased it." Sixty years after the original headline appeared a variation was successfully being used by S&S Mills Carpet to sell carpets. Their headline:

"My husband laughed when I ordered our carpet through the mail. But when I saved 50% . . ."

Caples, a pioneer of the mail-order advertising industry, knew exactly how to tap the power of self-interest. His recommendation:

> First and foremost try to get self-interest into every headline you write. Make your headline suggest to readers that here is something they want. The rule is so fundamental that it would seem obvious. Yet the rule is violated every day by scores of writers.[38]

Benefits are more persuasive when they are specific and meaningful. In a study that evaluated 54 comparable sets of ads, the ones that included more specific benefits had a recall that was 1.22 times better than other ads.[39]

Remarkably, even experienced ad writers forget to make their benefits specific and meaningful. Another study of 480 full-page print ads showed only 31 percent of the ads mentioned specific, meaningful benefits.[40]

Research also suggests that you should limit the number of benefits you claim for a product or service. When customers start to detect persuasive intent in a message they become increasingly skeptical.

A study by two marketing and behavioral science professors, Kurt Karlson of Georgetown University and Suzanne Shu of the University of California, Los Angeles, measured the number of positive claims prospects would consider before they became skeptical.

The professors found that customers are receptive to persuasive messages that contain up to three positive claims. But every claim made after three triggers leads to increasing levels of skepticism.

The takeaway is for messages that are clearly persuasive, it pays to limit yourself to your three highest impact claims.[41]

In his book *In Defense of Food*, Michael Pollen distills his advice into one three part maxim: Eat food. Not too much. Mostly plants."[42] The advice is compelling and memorable.

According to Ira Kalb, a professor of marketing at the Marshall School of Business at the University of Southern California, "the brain likes choices but not too many choices."[43]

The power of personalization

To appeal to a person's self-interest a message has to be seen as relevant. To be seen as relevant the message has to be personalized. In a world where we are bombarded with generic content, we pay attention to information and requests that have been specifically designed for us while we ignore generic messages.

A study by the psychologists Diana Cordova and Mark Lepper dramatically illustrates the power of personalization.

The experiment was based on a math video game given to fourth and fifth grade students. The students were asked to solve a series of math problems. The first group of students was given a generic set of instructions at the start of the game.

The second group was given a set of instructions that had been specifically written for them using information from their answers to short questionaires. The customized instructions included mention of their birth date, the names of three close friends and the names of their favorite foods and toys. The students were then asked to rate the game on a scale of 1 to 7 for enjoyment.

When the instructions were not personalized students rated the game 2.9.

In contrast, the students gave the game with a personalized introduction a 5.42. They were also twice as likely to stay after school to play the game. The students also scored 30 percent higher on a later math test. Cordova and Lepper found personalization increases levels of intrinsic motivation.

Because students understood how the information related to them, they were willing to put in the extra effort required to solve the really tough math problems.

Personalization also increased what Cordova and Lepper called "perceived competence." The students, when exposed to personalized information, became convinced they could excel at the game and as a result were more likely to persevere.[44]

Bernartzi and Lehrer report that in "study after study messages tailored to the individual . . . are far more effective at gaining attention and triggering behavior change."[45]

The good news for message makers working in the digital age is that it is now possible with smart software, algorithms and Big Data to customize Internet audiences of millions at low cost.[46]

Visual personalization

Danny Kalish is the co-founder of Idomoo, a startup that pioneered the use of customized videos.

Kalish started the company when he was convinced that people rarely have the time or concentration to read a complicated message. Kalish says digital personalization allows you to get "the scale of a broadcast and a success rate that compare to a one-on-one conversation." Kalish has built up a portfolio of successful case studies. A personalized video for a bank increased loan applications by 70 percent. The explanatory video for a large cable company reduced the number of service center calls by 30 percent.[47]

Kalish is a great believer in video superiority compared to text. If a picture is worth a thousand words then a personalized picture might be worth a thousand pictures. And a personalized video might be worth many personalized pictures.[48]

The power of a personalized email subject line

"Remember that a person's name is to that person the sweetest and most important sound in any language."

—Dale Carneigie,
How to Win Friends and Influence People

Psychologists have long known we positively and automatically react when we hear our own name.

In a new study three researchers from Stanford University and the University of Chicago tested what happens to consumer engagement and behavior when you add the recipient's first name into the subject line of an email.

In five experiments the authors analyzed consumer responses to 2.5 million emails.

The main company tested sells U.S.$1000 CFA and CPA test preparation packages.

The recipients were nearly 20 percent more likely to open an email when it had their name in the subject line. This generated almost a 31 percent boost in sales leads and a 17 percent reduction in the number of consumers who unsubscribed.

The firm values each lead at $100. The company was so impressed by the results it decided to immediately add recipients' names in the subject lines of all their marketing emails.[49]

IS YOUR MESSAGE APPEALING?

4. DIFFERENTIATION Is your message highly differentiated from others?

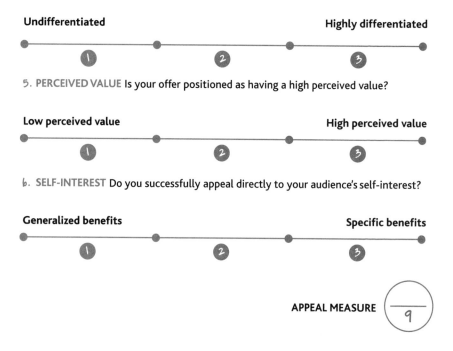

Undifferentiated　　　　　　　　　　　**Highly differentiated**

1　　　　　　　2　　　　　　　3

5. PERCEIVED VALUE Is your offer positioned as having a high perceived value?

Low perceived value　　　　　　　　**High perceived value**

1　　　　　　　2　　　　　　　3

6. SELF-INTEREST Do you successfully appeal directly to your audience's self-interest?

Generalized benefits　　　　　　　　　　**Specific benefits**

1　　　　　　　2　　　　　　　3

APPEAL MEASURE　　9

" There is only one way under high heaven to get anybody to do anything. And that is by making the other person want to do it."

—Dale Carnegie

4.

Unexpected

Surprising, Intriguing, and Seductive

T he attentional hotspots in customers' brains have adapted to our message-saturated environments by developing mental radars and machine guns to detect and shoot down unwanted messages.

To get under the radar, advertisers have responded by doing the unexpected.

In one ingenious campaign, Folgers coffee turned manhole covers in New York City into giant mugs of hot coffee. Painted images of the dark liquid in a round cup were fitted over the manhole covers. They then placed holes in the covers that emitted steam.

When pedestrians walked past in the morning they were greeted by the illusion that there were enormous cups of coffee embedded below street level.[50]

Unexpected messages are surprising, intriguing and seductive.

THE THREE UNEXPECTED CRITERIA

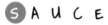 **S** A U C E

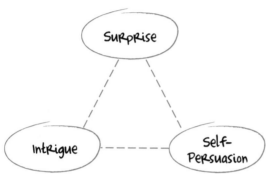

Unexpected messages are surprising

We ignore the expected and familiar. Once our brains become habituated to seeing something familiar we no longer give it attention. Surprise cuts through. We remember surprising occurrences.

Our brain craves novelty. Shoppers are attracted by stores that constantly update, rotate and refresh their stock displays. That's why they flock to fast fashion stores like Zara, who constantly change their selections.

Kmart's "Ship My Pants" ad is a clever example of novelty. The ad offers free shipping for items not available

in its stores. The ad begins with a customer replying to a
Kmart salesperson's news of free shipping with "I just might
ship my pants!"

The ad was designed to shock, amuse and turn
the mundane act of shopping into a slightly titillating
experience. It worked. YouTube views of the ad reached
twenty million within four months. YouTube thumbs-up
votes outscored thumbs-down votes by 25 to 1.[51]

The UK TV channel G2 was struggling to attract views
from its target audience of young males.

Its ad agency suggested changing the channel's name to
Dave. No UK Channel had ever used a first name before.
Dave was also informative about the target market and the
personality of the channel.

Dave's slogan was "the home of witty banter". People
had no trouble remembering that name and spontaneous
awareness jumped from two percent to thirty-two percent in
about six months. The ad campaign was highly successful
in attracting new viewers and won an IPA award.[52]

Unexpected messages are intriguing

While surprise is the key to grabbing attention, intrigue
is the key to holding it. Mysteries intrigue us. In 1951 on

the way to an advertising shoot for a small shirt company, David Ogilvy—now affectionately called the Father of Advertising—purchased several eye patches at a five and dime drugstore for 50 cents each. "Just shoot a couple of these to humor me" he told the photographer.

The resulting ad showed a "slender, haughty, mysteriously one eyed male model in a white dress shirt." The ad was accompanied by a long description of the shirt's benefits and appeared in the *New Yorker*.

Who was this man with an eye patch and how did he get it? American men were intrigued. Within a week C.F. Hathaway's entire shirt stock sold out. Hathaway had been making shirts for 116 years and was little noticed. Suddenly it was the number one selling dress shirt in the world.[53]

"The man in the Hathaway Shirt" has gone down in history and is probably the most famous print ad of all time. Before long companies ran ads featuring eye patches on babies, dogs and even cows.

To create mystery and intrigue and hold its readers attention, Ricoh the copier company ran a fresh two-page ad for its copier. The first page read:

Would you tolerate an employee who is anti-social, temperamental, abuses power, wastes office supplies, antagonizes other employees, requires professional help, and makes a habit of taking unscheduled vacations?

The next page read,

Then fire your copy machine.[54]

Unexpected messages are much more powerful when they use self-persuasion

There are just two ways to present a persuasive message. You can use direct persuasion—powerful arguments and evidence to convince a customer to buy—or you can use self-persuasion to help customers generate their own conclusions. When influencers help their buyers to generate their own conclusions, buyers commit faster and for longer.

Today's empowered, informed and demanding customers are becoming increasingly resistant to all forms of direct persuasion. Self-persuasion works because it reduces or eliminates buyer resistance. Customers don't argue with their own reasons.

In their book *Hidden Persuasion*, Marc Andrews, Dr. Matthijs van Leeuwen and Dr. Rick van Baaren compare

33 psychological influence techniques for effectiveness in advertising. They call self-persuasion the "holy grail" of persuasion research. Self-persuasion they say, "has repeatedly been demonstrated to trump any kind of given high-quality argument."[55]

The problem of consumer resistance is magnified when the market is already saturated with competing brands. This was the challenge the Cossette advertising agency faced when asked to help launch a new beer, *Molson Grand Nord*, onto the Canadian beer market.

Canadian beer drinkers already had a choice of over one thousand beers, so the ad campaign had to be high impact to stand any chance. Cossette's idea was simple but powerful: create a huge media campaign that would get buyers involved and tap into the power of self-persuasion.

Cossette created a series of commercials based on the adventures of two heroes. At the end of the first episode Molson asked viewers to choose an ending for the commercials. It proposed two different endings and asked viewers to vote for the one they preferred. A total of 992,000 people voted—that's 15 percent of all Canadians.

Two months later the ad agency called for another vote to choose the ending of a second commercial. To everyones' surprise there were 1.1 million votes. Everyone feared, without the novelty value of the first vote, the number of votes would plunge. Here is a brilliant example of what you can achieve when you use self-persuasion to involve customers in the decision process.[56]

IS YOUR MESSAGE UNEXPECTED?

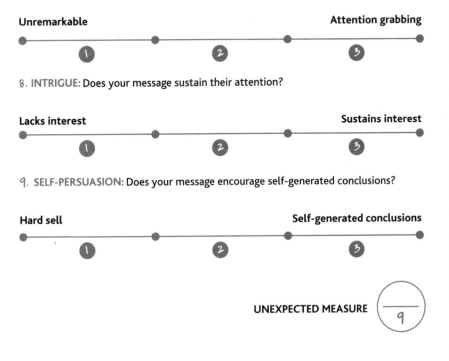

7. SURPRISE: Does your message grab your audience's attention?

Unremarkable   Attention grabbing

1   2   3

8. INTRIGUE: Does your message sustain their attention?

Lacks interest   Sustains interest

1   2   3

9. SELF-PERSUASION: Does your message encourage self-generated conclusions?

Hard sell   Self-generated conclusions

1   2   3

UNEXPECTED MEASURE   9

"To be persuasive, we must be believable; to be believable, we must be credible; to be credible, we must be truthful."

—Edward R. Murrow

5.

Credible

Trusted, Transparent, and Verifiable

W e live in a world where distrust of products and companies is endemic. So it is critical for your message to be credible. If customers distrust your company or message, then they discount everything you say.

If you exaggerate or claim you're the leader or finest in quality when the customer has a different view, you have a credibility problem.

Take Avis Rental Cars. For years Avis promoted its high quality. Claims of "Finest in rent-a-cars" advertisements simply didn't ring true. How could they have the finest rent-a-car service when Hertz was clearly the market leader?

Then Avis admitted it was No. 2. The advertisement declared, "Avis is No. 2. We try harder."

The advertising claims were now credible. Avis, who had lost money for 13 straight years, suddenly began to make money.[57]

"Candor is very disarming," say Al Ries and Jack Trout. "Every negative statement you make about yourself is instantly accepted as a truth. Positive statements, on the other hand, are looked at as dubious at best. Especially in an advertisement."[58]

```
     Credible messages
are trusted, transparent
     and verifiable.
```

THE THREE CREDIBLE CRITERIA

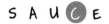

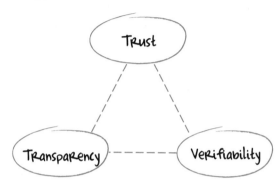

Credible messages are trusted

Popular wisdom says you need to build a trusted brand in order to get your customers to spend. But building a strong brand from scratch takes time and usually takes tens of millions of advertising dollars.

In the first quarter of 2013, a relatively unknown Taiwanese computer company called ASUS reached the number three position in worldwide tablet shipments with almost no initial brand awareness and without investing heavily in its brand.

In the old days, consumers used their past experience with a brand as a "key quality proxy." If you owned an HP computer you would use your experience with it to conclude that new HP models must be good.

But today you can access much better information about multiple computer makers, be they an HP, Dell or ASUS. You can go to a review site such as CNET or gadget.com and read reviews by experts and regular users.

When ASUS launched the Eee PC in 2007, geek bloggers fell in love with the dirt cheap $399 netbook. The device from a company virtually unknown in the United States sold almost five million units.[59]

"When quality can be quickly assessed, people are less hesitant to try something new, which means that newcomers like ASUS can enjoy lower barriers to entry," write Itamar Simson and Emanuel Rosen in *Absolute Value: What Really Influences Customers in the Age of (Nearly) Perfect Information*.[60]

We pay attention to, and act on, messages we trust. Neilson's 2013 survey of global trust in advertising and brand messages reports "believability is key in advertising effectiveness" and "trust and action often go hand in hand."[61]

So who do we trust? According to Edelman's highly regarded Trust Barometer, the source trusted by the majority is "people like me."

Before the Internet, people like me would have been an intimate network of friends and acquaintances. But social media has massively amplified "the people like me" and given it a megaphone.

We also trust information sources from friends, acquaintances and review sites much more than marketer-generated information. This is not surprising given the widespread distrust of business.

We trust experts. A decade ago, most peoples' access to experts was limited to magazines or newspaper columns. Today's top experts are a few clicks away and their recommendations are amplified by social media.

Credible messages are transparent

In 1913 *The London Times* ran the following ad:

Men wanted for hazardous journey. Small wages, bitter cold, long months of darkness, constant danger, safe return doubtful. Honour and recognition in case of success.

The ad attracted 5,000 applications for a crew of 27 on Shackleton's trip to the Antarctic.[62]

Advertising agency Doyle Dane Bernbach (DDB) used

the "law of candor" to create a remarkable campaign for Volkswagen, starting in 1960.

Many of the advertisements took the novel approach of knocking the product. Here are some of the headlines used:

- ▶ Ugly is only skin-deep
- ▶ Think small
- ▶ Lemon
- ▶ The 1970 VW will stay ugly longer.

The campaign was built around what the Beetle actually was: small, simple, economical, reliable and (except to VW addicts) ugly. In 1968 the VW Beetle sold 423,000 units in the United States—more than any other single automobile ever sold. The campaign's success is even more remarkable when you consider that the American market was at the time dominated by big gas-guzzling cars.

Bill Bernbach had a simple attitude to truth in advertising:

The truth isn't the truth until people believe you, and they can't believe you if they don't know what you're saying, they can't know what you're saying if they don't listen to you, and they won't listen to you if you're not interesting, and you won't be interesting unless you say things imaginatively, originally, freshly.[63]

Credible messages are verifiable

In the 1960s, "think small" was a brave call in an age of gas guzzling cars. In 2010 Volkswagen launched a global "think blue" campaign with the goal of becoming the world's most environmentally sustainable car manufacturer. VW promoted its "clean diesel" technology, which promised high mileage and low emissions without sacrificing performance. One ad campaign shows older ladies, in a Passat, arguing about whether diesel fuel is "sluggish and stinky". A Jetta ad says the car's engine is "painstakingly engineered without comprise".

VW was lying. In September 2015 Volkswagen admitted it had installed software in 11 million diesel cars to cheat emissions tests, allowing cars to "spew far more deadly pollutants than regulations allowed."

Consumers responded with outrage. VW's shares slumped and Martin Winterkorn, Volkswagen's chief executive and other high senior executives were forced to resign. In the space of 24 hours Volkswagen had gone from a brand people could trust to one that lied and cheated. The brand that had set out to become the world's most eco-friendly car had become a "big hypocrite."[64]

If you make a fact-based claim you should be able to support the facts by providing the source of evidence. When facts are verifiable, people become confident even if they don't bother to check your claim.

Shoppers are increasingly attracted to shopping on websites that include product reviews. Websites that don't include reviews cause customers to ask "What are they trying to hide?"

Verifiable evidence is persuasive. An analysis of advertising that looked at multiple studies in which some arguments provided sources and others did not, found the inclusion of sources led to higher persuasion in 17 of the 23 comparisons and it increased ratings of credibility in 7 of 11 comparisons.[65]

In a further study, the researchers found recall for verifiable ads was 1.23 times better than the other ads. Supporting evidence can often be provided on the Internet, which gives interested customers a low-cost way to validate claims.[66]

IS YOUR MESSAGE CREDIBLE?

10. **TRUST:** Does your message communicate you are trustworthy?

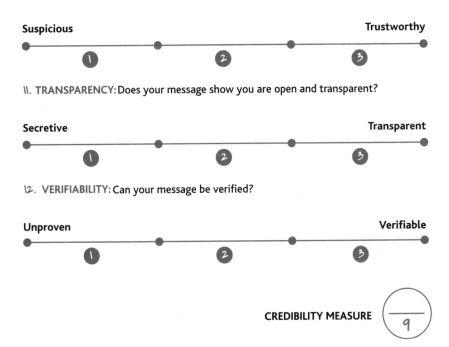

Suspicious   **Trustworthy**

①   ②   ③

11. **TRANSPARENCY:** Does your message show you are open and transparent?

Secretive   **Transparent**

①   ②   ③

12. **VERIFIABILITY:** Can your message be verified?

Unproven   **Verifiable**

①   ②   ③

CREDIBILITY MEASURE   9

**The advantage of the emotions
is that they lead us astray."**

—Oscar Wilde

6.

Emotional

Warm, Arousing, and Plot-Driven

Whether you want someone to buy an ocean liner or a brand of tissues you need to appeal to their emotions. According to Canadian neurologist Donald Caine, "The essential difference between emotion and reason is that emotion leads to action while reason leads to conclusions."[67] Even the blandest of subjects can be infused with emotion if the right strings are pulled. Take Texas' brilliant and stunningly successful campaign to slash litter on its highways. The initial advertising campaign Texas officials used to try to reduce littering was a total failure. Most of litterers were aged 18-24 and ignored the calls to change their behavior.

Then officials changed the message to appeal to one of the core 18-24-year-old values. Most 18-24 year olds were very proud to be Texans. So the officials came up with a campaign that appealed to their pride in Texas. The campaign centered on a tough-talking slogan called "Don't Mess with Texas!"

Sports heroes such as Dallas Cowboy football players were featured in television ads where they picked up litter, crushed beer cans in their hands and muttered, "Don't Mess with Texas." Popular country music singer Willie Nelson also pushed the message.

The campaign was so successful at appealing to the emotional psyche of the target group that there is now a mini-industry that sells "Don't Mess with Texas" coffee mugs, decals and flags.

In 2006, "Don't Mess with Texas" was voted America's favorite slogan. In the first year of the campaign, litter in the state was reduced by 29 percent. In the first 6 years, visible roadside litter fell by 72 percent.[68]

> Emotional messages are warm, arousing and plot-driven.

THE THREE EMOTIONAL CRITERIA

Emotional messages have a high affective warmth

We describe friendly people as warm and unfriendly people as cold. Warm and cold are primal sensations that we first experience in the womb and over time begin to associate with emotional states.

In one clever experiment a psychologist casually asked participants to briefly hold a cup of hot coffee or a cup of iced coffee while they were heading to a room to fill out a survey.

On arrival they each read a description of a fictitious person. The survey described the person as intelligent, skillful, industrious, determined, practical and cautious.

They were then asked to rate the person as generous or ungenerous, caring or selfish, attractive or unattractive, strong or weak.

When the researchers looked at the results they found the participants who had held a cup of hot coffee rather than a cup of iced coffee rated the fictitious person as significantly warmer and more friendly.

"The brain" writes Adam Alter, a marketing professor at the Stern School of Business at New York University and author of *Drunk Tank Pink and Other Unexpected Forces That Shape How We Think, Feel and Behave,* "interprets physical and social warmth very similarly."[69]

Another experiment showed that "giving someone the *cold shoulder* can actually make the person perceive a reduction in temperature."[70]

Conquest, a London-based marketing consultancy has devised a way to measure warmth using a metaphor. To measure the impact of its marketing campaigns, Conquest asks consumers to use online avatars to show their attitudes toward particular brands.

Instead of asking consumers, "What do you think of Brand X?" Conquest instructs participants to "Move your

avatar to show how you feel about Brand X." The closer
the consumer moves the avatar, the "warmer" her feelings
for the brand.

According to Conquest, "the affective warmth generated
by an ad is predictive of its success in the marketplace."[71]

Emotional messages are high
in emotional arousal

Why do some messages get shared around? What makes
online content go viral? Wharton marketing professor Jonah
Berger has spent the last decade answering these questions.

In his ground-breaking book *Contagious: Why Things
Catch On,* Berger provides new insights on the power of
emotional messages—and how they spread.

Berger studied thousands of *New York Times* articles to
understand why certain pieces of online content get shared.
The short answer is *emotion.* "When we care about the
content," says Berger, "we share."[72]

Traditionally, marketing researchers have classified
emotional messages as positive and negative. Newspapers
have long believed negative messages are more viral.
Consider the old new adage "if it bleeds, it leads." Bad
news is supposed to generate more attention than good
news.[73]

Berger's research, however, found the key to whether a message was shared or goes viral was not whether it was negative or positive. The key to sharing was a factor that psychologists call *physiological arousal.*

What is physiological arousal? It is the feeling you experience when your sports team is on the verge of winning a grand final. You may have had a similar feeling when you heard a weird noise as you were walking home in the dark. Your pulse races, your palms sweat, your heart pounds.

Arousal, writes Berger, "is a state of activation and readiness for action. Evolutionarily it comes from our ancestors' reptilian brains." Physiological arousal motivates a fight-or-flight response that helps us catch food or flee from predators. Arousal kindles our emotional fire.[74]

Some emotions, such as anger and excitement, are high arousal. When we're angry we yell at people; when we are excited we want to take action rather than sit around.

However, other emotions like sadness and contentment stifle action. Think about when people are content, they relax. When people are sad, they sit around.

Berger found content that makes us angry gets shared. When Dave Carroll of the group Sons of Maxwell watched

EMOTIONAL MESSAGE IMPACT MATRIX

	HIGH AROUSAL	LOW AROUSAL
Positive	Awe Excitement Amusement (Humor)	Contentment
Negative	Anger Anxiety	Sadness

Jonah Berger, *Contagious: Why Things Catch On*, Simon & Schuster, 2013

on in horror as United Airlines staff roughly tossed his treasured guitars through the air and later discovered his $3,500 guitar had been smashed, he shared his feelings on a YouTube video clip entitled "United Breaks Guitars."

Within ten days the video had 3 million views and 140,000 comments. Within four days of the video showing, the United stock price fell 10 percent or roughly $180 million.[76]

Awe is a high-arousal emotion. A clip from Susan Boyle's uplifting performance of "I Dreamed a Dream" on *Britain's Got Talent* amassed over 100 million views on YouTube.[77]

Understanding physiological arousal is the key to understanding why people share emails, articles or messages.

Emotional messages have a plot-driven storyline

The French poet Jacques Prévert was walking past a blind man displaying a sign "Blind man without a pension."

Prévert paused. He inquired how was he making out? Were people generous? Not really the man replied. "Some people but most just keep walking."

"Could I borrow your sign?" Prévert asked. The man said yes. The poet took the sign, turned it over and wrote a message. The next day he returned to talk to the blind man. "How are you doing?" he asked. "Great", the blind man replied. "I've never received so much money in my life."

On the sign Prévert had written: "Spring is coming, but I won't see it."[78]

Lisa Cron, the author of *Wired for Story* says "Recent breakthroughs in neuroscience reveal that our brain is hardwired to respond to story; the pleasure we derive from a well told story is nature's way of seducing us in to paying attention to it."[79]

Emotions move us and the best way to trigger an emotion is to tell a story.

Paul Zak is a neuroeconomist at Claremont Graduate University. In one study Zak made a short film describing the true story of Ben, a two-year-old dying of terminal cancer and his father John Doe. His life is largely uneventful until he discovers Ben has cancer.

Ben, however, doesn't know he has cancer and is dying. The story is about Ben's father's struggle to be happy around Ben; even though he knows that his sadness deprives Ben of joy he could have. Ben's father describes his struggle and how he finds the courage to remain joyful around Ben and be grateful for the gift of his child's brief life.

Zak showed this film to hundreds of people. Before viewing he measured oxytoxin levels in their blood. Oxytoxin is the chemical that makes us more trustworthy and generous. The film caused these levels to rise and half the group donated money to a childhood cancer charity.

Then Zak showed another group a different film showing a hairless Ben and his father visiting a zoo. It is clear Ben has cancer. Ben's father calls him "Miracle Boy." But there's no story arc. We're just viewing a father and son having a fun day at the zoo. This time the viewer's brain chemistry barely changed. They donated very little money.

Zak's research found the stories that cause our brains to release oxytoxin follow the classic story structure:

- ▶ John is living a normal life until he is hit by a setback—in this case the tragic news of Ben's brain tumor.
- ▶ John finds himself in conflict. Things get bad and then things turn worse as John struggles to deal with Ben's impending death.
- ▶ Finally, John faces his conflict and finds the inner strength to be grateful for Ben's brief but tragic life and is changed forever.[80]

In a later study to test the effects of different ads on donations, Zak's team sprayed oxytoxin into the nose of some of his subjects. Their donations were more than 50 percent greater and they gave to 57 percent more causes.[81]

Our response to stories depend heavily on the ending. "We absolutely love happy endings."

Predicting the success of Superbowl ads

Keith Queensbury is a marketing professor at Johns Hopkins University. For two years he studied 100 Superbowl ads to determine what, if anything, predicted how successful the ad would be. He found the key to a commercial's success was whether or not it had a dramatic storyline.

An interviewer for the *Johns Hopkins Magazine* challenged Queensbury to predict based on his findings which ad in the 2013 Superbowl would rate highest. His prediction was the Budweiser spot about the friendship of a puppy and a horse. "Budweiser" he said "loves to tell stories. And people love them." He was spot on. The ad rated highest on both *USA Today's* Ad Meter and Hulu's Ad Zone.[82]

Facebook research conducted with social media advertising technology firm Adaptly tested two comparable campaigns.

The first one, a sustained call to action, featured Facebook ads that used creative content and images focused strictly on generating email subscriptions.

The second campaign featured different "sequenced" ads that first told the brand story and then provided product information before inviting people to sign up.

Ads for both campaigns ran in the Facebook News Feed to similar audiences.

The researchers found the story-led sequence of ads generated 87 percent more people visiting the landing page and 56 percent more email subscriptions.[83]

IS YOUR MESSAGE EMOTIONAL?

13. AFFECTIVE WARMTH Does your message communicate you are engaging and warm?

Cold   **Warm**

①   ②   ③

14. EMOTIONAL AROUSAL Does your message generate high emotional arousal?

Low arousal   **High arousal**

①   ②   ③

15. STORY LINE Does your message have a plot-driven story line?

Facts and figures   **Plot-driven**

①   ②   ③

EMOTIONAL MEASURE $\frac{\quad}{9}$

SAUCE can be pictured
as a radar chart or
a heat gauge.

RADAR CHART

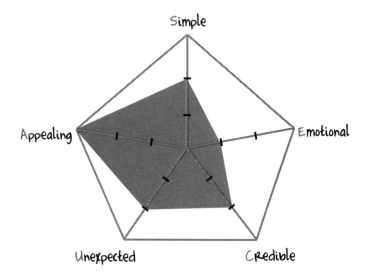

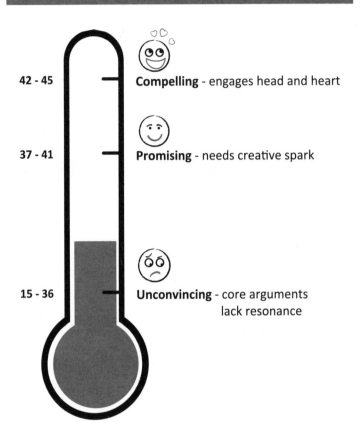

HEAT GAUGE

42 - 45 — **Compelling** - engages head and heart

37 - 41 — **Promising** - needs creative spark

15 - 36 — **Unconvincing** - core arguments
lack resonance

Most sales and marketing messages fail the SAUCE test

If you judge the success of a sales or marketing message by its ability to generate persuasive punch, only a small percentage succeed. 80 to 90 percent of the messages we have analyzed for large companies fail the SAUCE test.

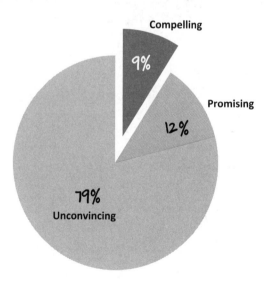

JUST 9 PERCENT OF MARKETING AND SALES COMMUNICATIONS PACK A PERSUASIVE PUNCH

Compelling
9%

Promising
12%

79%
Unconvincing

" When dealing with people, remember you are not dealing with creatures of logic, but with creatures of emotion, creatures bristling with prejudice and motivated by pride and vanity."

—Dale Carnegie

7.

The SAUCE Persuasive Impact Test

Instructions

- ▶ Select the message you wish to measure for persuasive impact.
- ▶ Use the SAUCE set of fifteen questions to calculate the total SAUCE score of your message (out of 45).
- ▶ Plot the individual scores for each of the five SAUCE criteria onto the radar gap analysis chart.
- ▶ Transfer your total SAUCE score onto the SAUCE Heat Gauge.
- ▶ Use the SAUCE criteria and guidelines to sharpen your message until it packs the necessary persuasive punch needed to successfully influence your audience.

TEST FOR SIMPLICITY

I. ONE CENTRAL TRUTH Has your message been stripped down to one central truth?

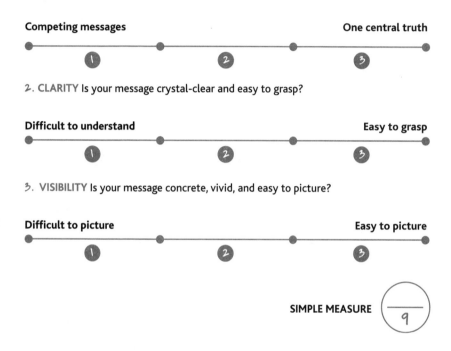

Competing messages   **One central truth**

2. CLARITY Is your message crystal-clear and easy to grasp?

Difficult to understand   **Easy to grasp**

3. VISIBILITY Is your message concrete, vivid, and easy to picture?

Difficult to picture   **Easy to picture**

SIMPLE MEASURE $\frac{}{9}$

TEST FOR APPEAL

4. DIFFERENTIATION Is your message highly differentiated from others?

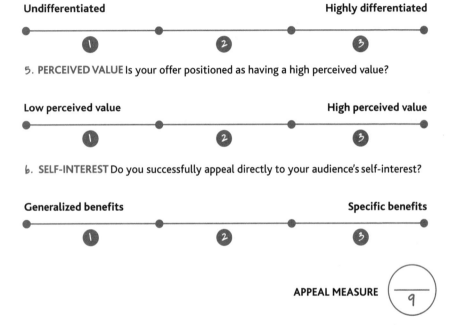

Undifferentiated   **Highly differentiated**

1   2   3

5. PERCEIVED VALUE Is your offer positioned as having a high perceived value?

Low perceived value   **High perceived value**

1   2   3

6. SELF-INTEREST Do you successfully appeal directly to your audience's self-interest?

Generalized benefits   **Specific benefits**

1   2   3

APPEAL MEASURE   9

TEST FOR CREDIBILITY

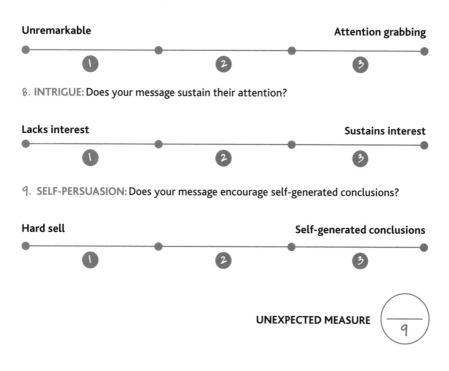

7. SURPRISE: Does your message grab your audience's attention?

Unremarkable   **Attention grabbing**

①   ②   ③

8. INTRIGUE: Does your message sustain their attention?

Lacks interest   **Sustains interest**

①   ②   ③

9. SELF-PERSUASION: Does your message encourage self-generated conclusions?

Hard sell   **Self-generated conclusions**

①   ②   ③

UNEXPECTED MEASURE $\dfrac{\quad}{9}$

TEST FOR TRUST

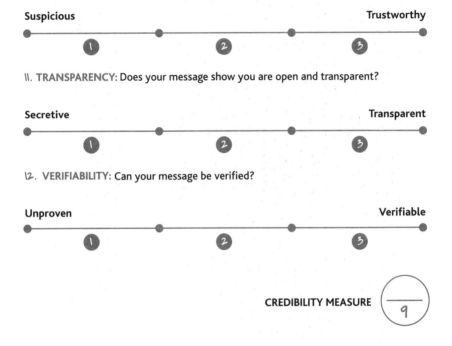

10. **TRUST:** Does your message communicate you are trustworthy?

Suspicious   Trustworthy

① ② ③

11. **TRANSPARENCY:** Does your message show you are open and transparent?

Secretive   Transparent

① ② ③

12. **VERIFIABILITY:** Can your message be verified?

Unproven   Verifiable

① ② ③

CREDIBILITY MEASURE ⬯9

TEST FOR EMOTION

13. AFFECTIVE WARMTH Does your message communicate you are engaging and warm?

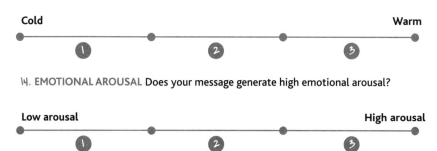

Cold   Warm

①   ②   ③

14. EMOTIONAL AROUSAL Does your message generate high emotional arousal?

Low arousal   High arousal

①   ②   ③

15. STORY LINE Does your message have a plot-driven story line?

Facts and figures   Plot-driven

①   ②   ③

EMOTIONAL MEASURE $\dfrac{}{9}$

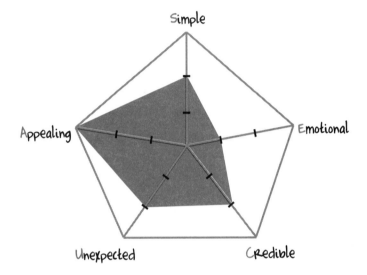

RADAR CHART

HEAT GAUGE

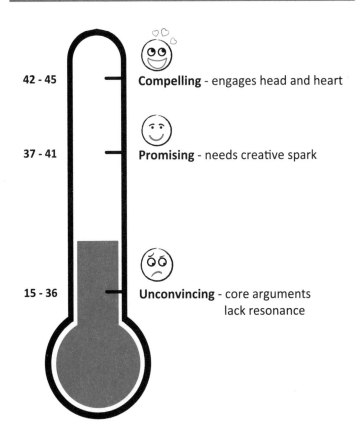

42 - 45   **Compelling** - engages head and heart

37 - 41   **Promising** - needs creative spark

15 - 36   **Unconvincing** - core arguments
                lack resonance

Part II

Lessons from the Frontline

8.

Predict,
Test, Learn

Lessons from J.C. Penney

J.C. Penney hires Apple's marketing genius

In 2011 J.C. Penney, despite a brand history that stretched back 111 years and over 1000 stores dotted across the United States, was stagnating. It was no longer the store of choice for middle-income families. Revenues and profits in 2011 were down from what they had been 15 years earlier. Though profitable, Penney was losing ground to rivals like Macy's and Kohls.

To lure customers, the fading brand became addicted to continuous sales and aggressive discounts, fueled by coupons. In 2011, the company ran a staggering 590 promotions. Seventy-two percent of its goods sold at discounts of 50 percent or more. Less than one percent of its goods sold at full price.[84]

To engineer a turnaround, Penney hired retail superstar Ron Johnson as its new CEO from Apple. At Apple, Johnson had worked with Steve Jobs to turn the Apple Store into one of most profitable retailers on the planet. Apple store sales averaged $6,000 a square foot compared to $156 at J.C. Penney.

Before moving to Apple, Johnson's marketing talents had transformed Target from an undifferentiated discount store into a chic affordable destination.

On the same day Johnson was announced as Penney's incoming CEO its stock soared 17.5 percent. The market believed Johnson was a retail genius with a Midas touch. To make up for the shares Johnson lost by leaving Apple, Penney issued Johnson $50 million dollars in stock.

Fair and square pricing

To replace J.C. Penney's depleted sales, discounts and coupons Johnson introduced Fair and Square pricing that emphasized everyday, low prices and just a few major sales each year.

At the same time, Johnson ended what was the "9" ending sales prices. For example, instead of discounting a pair of sandals listed at $29.99 down to $14.99, he listed the prices at an everyday price of $15.00.

High-profile ads featuring popular comedienne Ellen DeGeneres heavily promoted Fair and Square as a more ethical way to do business. Johnson also eliminated all coupons.

While Fair and Square prices eliminated a lot of confusion over value, Johnson was careful to ensure that the absolute level of discounts was not cut. But J.C. Penney's core customers hated the changes. In just 16 months the company's sales fell by 25 percent. Nineteen thousand staff lost their jobs and the stock fell by nearly 50 percent.

In April 2013, after little more than 12 months as CEO, Johnson was fired.[85]

So what went wrong?

For a start, Johnson assumed that what had worked at Target and Apple stores would work at a mid-tier department store where the customers were addicted bargain hunters.

Johnson rolled out his plans without testing his changes first.

When Johnson first floated plans for the chain's radical makeover, he was asked about the possibility of trying the new pricing strategies on a limited test basis. Johnson reportedly shot down the idea, responding, "We didn't test at Apple."

Bill Ackman, the board member and activist investor who had led the call to hire Johnson in the first place, noted "people seemed to be happier at buying something at 50 percent off that costs $50 as opposed to being marked at $40 and there being no discount."[86]

Johnson wrongly believed constant price promotions caused J.C. Penney's customers confusion, uncertainty and mistrust. Price promotions were in fact reducing the pain of buying. For years stores like J.C. Penney's have conditioned their buyers to look forward to special deals, coupons and discounts. Indeed it was the price promotions and the bargain hunt that attracted consumers to J.C. Penney stores.[87]

Why people don't buy

Mark Ellwood, the author of *Bargain Fever*, says, "These are not women who feel taken advantage of by coupons and deals. To them, there's the thrill of the hunt—it's hunting and gathering with a credit card. No consumers have been complaining about discounts."[88]

Johnson might have learned from rival Macy's earlier experience when Macy's acquired May Co. in 2005. Macy's reduced the number of discounts. Sales and the stock price fell. After Macy's managers backed down and restored the discounts, Macy's chief financial officer said, "People love these coupons. They love thinking they got us."

Isn't $14.99 the same as $15?

One of the features of Johnson's Fair and Square pricing was doing away with the traditional practice of 9-ending prices. One advertisement sent featured Ellen Degeneres ridiculing a sales person for the "deceptive nature of $14.99 prices (as opposed to the simplicity of $15.)"[89]

Research shows, however, that "9-ending prices and sales signs have a strong impact over shopping behaviors." Savvy retailers know that 9-endings do increase the "value perceptions of their merchandise." 9-endings "can serve as 'sales signs' on their own and thus make the price seem more attractive than it is."

"Processing price information activitates the same region of the brain as that which processes physical pain."

When customers encounter prices they think are excessive, another region of the brain—the insula—activates. The insula activates when we "smell something bad, see something disgusting or anticipate a painful shock."

Remarkably, insula activation corrrectly predicts whether someone will buy or not buy an item. "The greater the insula activation the less likely the item will be bought."[90]

The power of A/B testing

In 2007, Dan Siroker took a leave of absence from Google to join Barack Obama's election campaign team as a head digital advisor.

The new media team's greatest challenge was to turn their campaign's website visitors into subscribers and convert them into donors.

Coming from Google, Siroker was a big believer in A/B testing.

In an A/B test of a web page, a group of users are diverted to a modified version of a web page and their behavior is compared to the bulk of users still going to the standard site.

If the new (B version) generates more clicks and more subscriptions or donations, it will replace the original (or A version). If the new version is inferior then it is rejected.

A/B testing allows every element of a message—packaging and design, color, layout, image selection and text—to be tested and proven.

Guided by Siroker, Obama's new media team broke the campaign website's visitor page into component parts and came up with a number of alternatives to test.

For the action button they tested three new word choices—"Learn More," "Join Us Now" and "Sign Up Now."

The "Learn More" generated 18.6 percent more signups than the default of "Sign Up." When tested with a black and white photo of the Obama family it outscored the default turquoise picture by 13.1 percent. Together, the family image and the "Learn More" button increased sign-ups by a remarkable 40 percent.

Obama's media team consisted of a number of persuasion-savvy professionals. Yet virtually all were wrong when it came to predicting which combination of button text and support image would work best. Nearly all of them believed a video of Obama speaking at a rally would outpunch any photo. But in fact, the video performed worst. If the media team had retained "Sign Up" as the button text and swapped out the photo for the video—the sign-up rate would have slipped to 70 percent of the baseline. This is a compelling example of why A/B testers believe so strongly that assumptions tend to be wrong.[91]

Before Siroker came to the Obama campaign, the HiPPO syndrome reigned supreme. A/B disciples describe a decision-making environment where opinions count for more than data as HiPPO—"highest paid person's opinion." Google analytics expert Avinash Kaushik believes "most websites suck because HiPPOS create them."[92]

Testing allows you to monitor changes in customer preferences. At the gaming network IGN, for example, executives found that clear, crisp writing was outpulling buzzwords (like free and exclusive) on parts of their homepage. In past years, the opposite had been true. Why? The IGB staff aren't sure. I suspect increasingly savvy online consumers are becoming more resistant to overt sales speak.

After the Obama campaign Siroker launched his own A/B testing firm called Optimizely. Here is an outline of Optimzely's five stage A/B testing process.

1. Determine the conversion you want to improve. The conversion would be as simple as increasing the number of your email sign-ups.
2. Hypothesize the change. Generate reasons why you think the change will be more successful than the current one.
3. Identify the variables and create variations. Use your A/B testing software to make the desired changes to an element of your website or app.

4. Run the experiment. Kick off your experiment and wait for the visitors to engage. Your visitors will be randomly assigned to either the control or the variation of your experiment.

5. Measure the results. Once your experiment is complete, analyze the results. A/B testing software will present the data from the experiment so it highlights the difference between how the two versions of a page perform and whether there is a statistically significant difference.[93]

If your variation is a winner you can apply the findings to other pages and keep iterating. If it's a failure, treat the experiment as a learning experience.

Optimizely reports the A/B tests you make will vary according to your industry. For example, if you are a technology company who needs to increase the number of high-quality leads for your sales team, you might want to increase the number of free-trial users.

You might test:

► Lead firm components
► Free-trial signup flow
► Home page messaging and the call to action.[94]

The value of multiple tests

At age 14 Zachary Sobiech, a happy-go-lucky teenager, learned he had osteosarcoma, a deadly cancer of the bones. Chemotherapy didn't work. But Zach bravely accepted his fate and lived life to the fullest. "You can either sit in the basement and wait," he said, "Or you can get out there and do some crazy stuff."

A filmmaker documented Zach's courageous and inspiring last days. It showed Zach living happily, hanging out with his family and playing music.

When the team at Upworthy, which was the fastest-growing U.S. media company, saw the film, they knew this was a story that needed to be shared. They believed *My Last Days* had the potential to go viral. The filmmaker had posted the documentary online with the headline, "My Last Days: Meet Zach Sobiech," but few viewers had clicked. So Upworthy retitled the video "We lost this kid 80 years too early. I'm glad he went out with a bang."[95]

Upworthy also sent the same video with a mix of headlines to *different* subscribers. The Upworthy team watched the feedback, measuring the percentage of people who clicked each headline and the number who shared it with their friends.

Here is a sample of the results:

HEADLINE
{ % LIFT }
We lost this kid 80 years too early. I'm glad he went out with a bang.
0%
The happiest story about a kid dying of cancer I've ever seen.
+28%
Cancer wasn't a death sentence for this kid. It was a wake up call.
-22%
This kid just died. What he left behind is wonderful.
+96%

The winning headline was:

This kid just died. What he left behind is Wondtacular.

A thumbnail photo—Zach and his girlfriend touching foreheads boosted the click-through another 69 percent. In the end, over 10 million people read Zach's story. [96]

9.

Make it Easy, Make it Effortless

Don't Make it Hard to Say Yes

Don't make it hard to say yes

Brian Wansink, professor of Consumer Behavior at Cornell University and author of the bestselling *Mindless Eating: Why We Eat More Than We Think*, studies what happens when choices are made easier or more difficult.

Wansink found that when healthy food was the easiest choice, for example by displaying it more prominently, we eat more of it.

Wansink, in one experiment, tested what happened to ice cream consumption in a cafeteria when a freezer cabinet containing ice cream was left open. People could always see the ice cream when the lid was open. When the lid was open 30 percent took an ice cream. When the lid was closed only 14 percent bothered to make the tiny effort required.

To make healthy eating the norm Wansink argues you need to make healthy eating mindless. For example: put healthy options in prominent places in school cafeterias. Make healthy food easier to reach. Use lighting to display healthy foods more prominently. In other words, "make healthy food the easiest choice."[97]

Reducing the consumption of M&Ms

Google conducted a similar experiment to Wansink's to see if they could reduce the consumption of M&Ms. The M&Ms in their New York office used to be in baskets. So instead they put them in bowls with lids.

The lids required very little effort to lift, but it reduced the number of M&Ms consumed in their New York office by 3 million a month.[98]

Harnessing the power of default

In 2003, Dan Goldstein and Eric Johnson published a study of organ consent rates across 11 European countries. The rates varied from 4.2 percent for Denmark to 99.9 percent for France.

What was the cause of the huge differences? Were there cultural factors? It didn't appear so. In Austria and Germany, neighboring countries with a common language, cultural similarities and a lot of shared history, the differences were huge. Organ donation consent rates in Austria were 99.8 percent, and in Germany were just 12 percent.

The researchers found the differences could be explained by a simple administrative procedure on a form.

The four countries with the lowest rates all required people to consent to organ donation. They all had to check a "yes" box.

The seven countries with the highest rates all required that people opt out of organ donation.

The tiny physical effort of checking boxes on a form and the mental effort required to go against the default meant people gravitated in mass toward the easy. [99]

Transforming business into an effortless experience

In their book, *The Effortless Experience, Conquering the New Battleground for Customer Loyalty*, authors Matthew Dixon, Nick Toman and Rick Delisi argue that service organizations create loyal customers primarily by reducing customer effort, that is, by helping them solve their problems quickly and easily.

The Effortless Experience is full of examples of how the customer experience can be made easier. Old Navy, for example, has made the experience of shopping with kids easier by lowering the heights of racks so that parents can see where their kids are. They've labeled the hooks in their changing rooms "Love it", "Like it" and "Not for me". The Old Navy hooks clarify choices and make the next step—buying—"simple and apparent."[100]

Revolutionizing banking in India

Just making a process easier can dramatically impact behavior. Until recently only 35.5 percent of Indian households actively maintained bank accounts. Then, in August 2014, the new prime minister launched *Pradhan Mantri Jan Dhan Yojana* (The Prime Minister's People Money Scheme). Five months later 106 million new bank accounts had been opened.

The account opening form had been simplified and the documentary requirement for proof of address had been relaxed.[101]

Reducing cognitive load

Effortful tasks tax our cognitive load. We favor decisions that require less mental effort.

Scientists use the term cognitive fluency "when they measure how easy it is to think about something." Cognitive fluency causes us to make choices that are easy to evaluate, rather than choose the one that offers us the greatest reward.

Brand expert Simon Bird writes that "famous, popular or preferred brands make choice effortless."

Brain scans show shoppers' brains show much less effort when choosing the number one brand. Strong brands, it seems, help the brain to "think less."[102]

Raising university attendance

University attendance rates among unrepresented groups in the United States rose by 8 percent when forms were filled and submitted on behalf of the applicant.[103]

Similar studies have found that we don't make the effort to pay into a retirement fund—even when our employer offers to match our contributions—unless the default option is set on yes.

Why? It's simply easier to do nothing, writes Maria
Konnikova, the author of *Mastermind: How to Think Like
Sherlock Holmes.*[104]

How to increase cab driver tips by 12 percent

In 2007, New York City forced cab drivers into taking credit
cards. During payment the passenger is presented with a
touch screen with three easy-to-choose defaults for tipping
20 percent, 25 percent and 30 percent.

When cabs were cash only, the average tip was roughly
10 percent. With the touchscreen, the tip percentage jumped
to 22 percent. The addition of three easy-to-touch buttons
resulted in $144 million of additional tips per year.[105]

So easy, a caveman could do it

Just focusing on the ease of doing business can be profitable.
Car insurance giant Geico's ad campaign, which has been
running since 2004, highlights the ease of using their website.
They picture Neanderthal cavemen. The supporting tagline
reads "So easy, a caveman could do it."[106]

10.

Message Magic in the Twenty-First Century

Lessons from BuzzFeed

n 2015 Fast Company named BuzzFeed the world's most innovative company for shaking up media across the globe.

BuzzFeed owns all the core ingredients of a modern media company. It has a global news team, its own video production studio, an inhouse creative ad agency plus a sophisticated data operation.

BuzzFeed was founded in 2006 but for much of that time it was little more than a single website. BuzzFeed CEO Jonah Peretti's eureka moment came in late 2014 when he realized that "people wouldn't want to leave their social apps." So Peretti radically changed his strategy. Instead of trying to lure eyeballs to its own website, the way most publishers do, BuzzFeed would publish original text images and video directly to where its audience already spent its time.[107]

Rather than write one definitive article and publish it on every platform (the defacto standard in the media business) BuzzFeed would tailor content specifically for the network and audience where it was being viewed.[108]

The lesson here for 21st century message makers is that where your customers hang out can change overnight and the media they respond to can change just as fast.

The results of the change proved remarkable. The company now pulls five billion monthly viewers. Over 50 percent come from video. The BuzzFeed video team currently produces 65 original videos a week. This is a startling number, given the video business barely existed two years ago. Traffic, in the meantime, to BuzzFeed's website "has remained steady—80 million people in the U.S. every month." That figure alone ranks it ahead of the *New York Times*, "even though as much as 75 percent of BuzzFeed's content is now published elsewhere."[109]

Media competitors look on in wonder at how BuzzFeed manages to consistently craft out a flood of content and ads that are shared so widely and every now and again go mega-viral.

The secret is its sophisticated data operation. All of BuzzFeed's articles are input into the data center and are analyzed for impact. The feedback determines how BuzzFeed creates, adapts and distributes its content and advertising. BuzzFeed, in short, is an adaptable, agile culture that learns fast and delivers faster than its competitors. It uses data to discover what its customers love and then monetizes it by delivering it. In the process, data transforms into dollars.[110]

Fast feedback means BuzzFeed can leverage and optimize the power of its most successful content. When a website article titled *"30 Awkward Moments Every Short Girl Understands"* launched it was turned into a YouTube video *("Ten Problems Only Short Girls Understand")* and later became the inspiration for a cartoon called *Trans Girl Problems* that ran on Facebook.[111]

While BuzzFeed, with a market value of near $11 billion, is an undoubted media success story, it does have a trust problem with its news and politics. *Fortune Magazine* reports, quoting a Pew Center survey (2014), that just four percent of millennials trust the site about politics.

The most trusted news entity was CNN, which 60 percent of millennials said they trusted. NBC News and the *New York Times* also scored highly. BuzzFeed was close to dead last.

BuzzFeed does worry about its reputation as a serious news provider. It has invested large sums in setting up a separate site for BuzzFeed news and has put more effort into publicizing hard-hitting investigative journalism.

ABC, NBC and CBS took time to build reputations as trusted news sources. Time will tell whether BuzzFeed can do the same.

11.

The Power
of Situations

How Context
Shapes the Way
We Behave

The power of context

Message makers have a habit of overestimating the importance of the personality of the person they are trying to influence and underestimating the power of the surrounding situation or context.

Sam Sommers, the author of *Situations Matter: Understanding How Context Transforms Your World*, tells us that "everyday . . . we overlook the enormous power of situations or context in our lives. Just as a museum visitor neglects to notice the frame around a painting, so do most people miss the influence of ordinary situations on the way they think and act."[112]

The good samaritan

To demonstrate the power of situations over personality in shaping behavior, two social psychologists, John Darley and Daniel Batson, set up a clever experiment involving divinity students at Princeton Theological Seminary.

A group of young seminarians were asked to prepare a sermon on the parable of the Good Samaritan to be later delivered in a nearby building.

While walking there the students passed a shabbily dressed actor slumped in a doorway. As each student passed by, the actor moaned and coughed. But only 40 percent of the divinity students helped in any way.

What explains this finding? Surprisingly, why did 60 percent of the students ignore the plea for help?

The researchers had divided the students into two groups. One group of students was told they had plenty of time to get to their appointment. Sixty-three percent of this group stopped to provide help. A second group was told they had to hurry because they were running late. Only 10 percent of this group helped.

The researchers concluded that the personalities of the divinity students had very little to do with whether or not they stopped to help. A situational factor—being in a hurry—was a much better predictor of helping behavior than personality type regardless of whether the person was kind or caring.[113]

The smell of a cookie

In another study testing the willingness to help others, researchers approached 116 people at an American shopping mall requesting change for a dollar.

Sixty percent of those who were standing in front of a Cinnabon or a Mrs. Fields Cookies agreed to the request. But less than 20 percent of the respondents who were standing outside clothing stores helped when asked.

Questioning revealed the smells emanating from the bakeries put those asked into a better mood, "and people are more helpful when they are happy."[114]

The fundamental attribution error

When we overestimate the extent to which people's personalities shape their behavior and underestimate the extent to which behavior is the product of situational influences we have fallen victim to what psychologists call the *fundamental attribution error* (FAE).

Thousands of research studies show humans "are highly susceptible to this error." It's a mistake all message makers need to guard against.[115]

Cultural context

Not all cultures pay equal attention to context. American, European and other Western cultures pay less attention to context than East Asian cultures.

Look at the image below. This is a still taken from a twenty-second video of an underwater scene.

If you're an American then you're likely to say "I saw three big fish swimming off to the left, they had darker fins and white bellies and vertical stripes on their backs."

Japanese people are much more likely to say, "I saw what looked like a stream, there were rocks and shells on the bottom, there were three big fish swimming off to the left."

Only after context is established, do the Japanese focus on what are the most important objects for Americans. In total, the Japanese reported seeing 60 percent more background objects than did the Americans. In other words, the Japanese pay more attention to the context or situation.[116]

In a related experiment, the social psychologist Takahiko Masuda asked Japanese and American college students to rate the expression of the central figures below.

Japanese students rate the central figure as less happy when he is surrounded by sad (or angry figures). The Americans were much less affected by the emotion of the surrounding figures.[117]

Situation management on steroids

If you want to study how experts in the science of situational management can influence every aspect of our behavior then visit a casino. Modern video gambling has been called "the most virulent strain of gambling in the history of man."

Machine gambling in Las Vegas

In a remarkable book, *Addiction By Design*, author Natasha Dow Schull describes how casinos have become irresistible addiction environments that entice and entrap unwitting and vulnerable gamblers.[118]

Until the mid 1980s casino floors were covered with green felt table games such as blackjack and craps. Today, the floors are covered in slot machines. Over 85 percent of industry profits come from machines.

Visiting a town like Las Vegas with its hundreds of thousands of tourists might make you think tourists are the big gamblers. Not so. Tourists are transient players. It is the local population who make up the largest percentage of valuable repeat players.

The steady repetition of machine play by locals at the dollar slots yield a better revenue stream than the episodic, high-rolling play of tourists who play at the green felt tables.

Over 80 percent of local gamblers belong to loyalty clubs. Their loyalty cards document and track their gambling habits, which are analyzed in minute detail. Some casinos have facial recognition software that enables a player's favorite machine to call out to her by name if cameras on the casino floor detect that she is headed toward the exit.[119]

The maze

Industry researchers have discovered the best-performing slot machines are those that are located within "insulated enclosures" tucked or hidden in "small alcoves, recesses and corners," or "sheltered in the "nooks and crannies."

Casinos are structured as mazes to steer gamblers toward a destination where they want to "stop, sit and play."

Every effort is made to keep patrons flowing toward the machines. Casino patrons slow down and have to think harder if they have to turn 90 degrees to get to a slot aisle.

So casinos are designed with uninterrupted, curvilinear pathways.

Curving starts outside the casino property. The entry to the property should beckon and invite and curve gently off the street or sidewalk.

Ideally there should be no right angles or stop signs. In one test, the change from a right angle of an entrance corridor to a slight curve increased the percentage who entered the casino from one-third to two-thirds.[120]

Aisles leading to gambling areas narrow gradually so walkers do not notice until "they suddenly find themselves" in the intimate world of gambling action.

Once patrons are seated at the gambling machines, the slot machines take over as the dominant force of guidance.

But even here the temperature, light, color, sound and aroma is controlled to produce an "experiential effect" that will immerse them "in the zone" and facilitate "contented imprisonment."[121]

Continuous gaming productivity

Slot machines are designed to keep patrons playing and immersed in the zone. Continuous gaming productivity is the goal.

Continuous gaming productivity involves three components—*accelerating* play, *extending* its duration and *increasing* the amount spent.[122]

Accelerating play

Speed is the critical element in the zone experience. When gamblers hold their speed steady they stay in the zone.

When gamblers used the old-style mechanical pull handles they could play up to 300 games an hour. Experienced video poker gamblers can now complete an astonishing 900 to 1,200 hands an hour.

As a consequence, the modern gaming machine has become "a very fast, money eating device." [123]

Extending the time on device

Casinos want to keep gamblers playing as long as "humanly possible." Modern machines are designed so that gamblers can play multiple games without ever having to leave their seats.

Machines have become sensory environments. Audio engineers have discovered ways of delivering sound technology that rewards steady play. Haptic feedback technology integrate touch sensations into the machine interface further improving the overall gaming experience.

Improvement in machine ergonomics has improved player comfort, further increasing time on device. Patrons who are physically and psychologically comfortable stay longer and spend more.[124]

Maintaining the flow of funds

To play continuously, gamblers need access to an uninterrupted flow of play funds.

As recently as the 1980s machine gamblers who had run out of money had to go to the ATM to get cash and then purchase rolls of coins at cashier cages.

The introduction of a cashless ticket-in/ticket-out (TITO) technology made coin payouts obsolete and increased the speed and magnitude of the play by 20 percent.

A number of jurisdictions already allow players to access extra credit while remaining at their gambling machine. It seems only a matter of time before the remaining jurisdictions follow. A company called Global Cash Access calls its device for accomplishing this "Stay-n-Play." [125]

Contrived to deceive

When a gambler plays blackjack, or a game of dice such as craps or roulette, the odds a player faces are apparent to him.

Early slot machines shared this attribute: There were generally three reels, each with a fixed number of slots with various symbols on them. Lining up the same symbol across all three reels triggered a payout.

When purely mechanical slots were replaced by computerized machines, it became possible for casinos to manipulate how the *apparent* odds are presented to a player, independently of the actual odds being offered.

Using a technique called clustering, a "disproportionate number of virtual stops are mapped to blank spaces just above or below the jackpot symbols." This enhances the "near miss" sensation among players and makes them want to continue to play. Clustering makes players believe the odds of success offered by the house are better than they actually are.

The manipulating of the odds means the casinos can afford to occasionally offer multi-million dollar jackpots, which is a key to attracting new gamblers.[126]

12.

The Confirmation Bias

The Mother of All Misconceptions

When buyers evaluate a new proposal they don't always judge it on its merits. They ignore or reinterpret new information that contradicts their existing views. For the most part they focus on information that confirms their current beliefs and explain away or disregard evidence that doesn't.

When we interpret new information so it reinforces our existing beliefs we have fallen victim to what social scientists call the confirmation bias.

In the mid 1990s Motorola's analog phones dominated the cell phone market, with a market share of 30 percent at its peak. So when U.S. carrier Sprint asked for a digital model phone, Motorola said no. Even though digital technologies were touted as the way of the future, Motorola ignored the evidence and put even more investment and effort into analog phones.

As a result, between 1998 and 2003 Motorola's share of the global mobile phone market fell by over 50 percent. During the same period, Nokia became the leader of the digital phone revolution. By 2001 it was capturing 70 percent of all the profits made in the industry. The Motorola story is a classic example of a company falling victim to the confirmation bias.[127]

The confirmation bias is so powerful it is called the mother of all misconceptions. Legendary investor Warren Buffett says, "What the human being is best at doing is interpreting all information so that their conclusions remain intact."[128]

The confirmation bias is tough to overcome because most people don't find it natural to do what is required to overcome it—"which is to deliberately seek answers that contradict their beliefs and preferences."[129]

The confirmation bias helps explain the old adage, "you never get a second chance to make a first impression." "Once an idea sets in your head, it often sets in concrete; you can break it but you may need a sledgehammer," explain Gary Belsky and Thomas Gilovich, the authors of *Why Smart People Make Big Money Mistakes.*[130]

We now know where in the brain the confirmation bias is processed, thanks to a brain scan (fMRI) study conducted at Emery University by Drew Western.

When we hold strong partisan beliefs on an issue we don't use the parts of the brain that normally engage during reasoning. Instead we engage our emotion circuits until we arrive at the conclusion we want. And when we resolve the conflict our brain delivers a reward in the form of a feel-good neurochemical hit, probably dopamine.[131]

Overcoming the confirmation bias

When people are emotionally committed to a position, presenting more information will rarely correct their misunderstanding. In fact, presenting more information can backfire and harden their position.

However, one intriguing study by Philip Fernbach, a University of Colorado business school professor, discovered a powerful technique for changing entrenched minds.

His study found that "If you ask people to justify their beliefs they tend to act as their lawyer or public relations managers and they don't move toward great moderation. However, if you ask people to explain in detail how the policies they support actually work, they discover how much they don't know—and they moderate their position."[132]

Fernbach started the study because he wanted to understand how it was possible that individuals could maintain such strong positions—on complex issues such as macroeconomics, health care and foreign relations—and yet seem to be so ill informed about the issues.

Fernbach believes people hold extreme policy positions because they suffer from an illusion of understanding. However, when you get people to explain the nuts and bolts of how a policy works you force them to acknowledge that they don't know as much about a policy as they initially thought.[132]

13.

Framing

It's Not What You Say— It's How You Say It

The Jesuit and the Benedictine

A Jesuit priest and a Benedictine monk shared a problem. Both were addicted chain smokers, and they had to spend large portions of their day praying all the while craving a smoke.

After talking about their problem they agreed to discuss it with their respective superiors and report back the following week.

When they met again, the Jesuit asked the Benedictine how the meeting had gone. "Disastrously," he replied. "I asked the abbot, 'Will you give me permission to smoke while I'm praying?' and he was furious. He gave me fifteen extra penances as a punishment for my irreverence. But you look happy, my brother, what happened to you?"

The Jesuit smiled. "I went to my rector, and asked, 'May I have permission to pray while I am smoking?' Not only did he give me permission, but he congratulated me on my piety."[133]

Like the Jesuit, successful persuaders know how to extract value out of every word by framing their message.

George Perkins reframes a negotiation

George Perkins—in case you don't know—was a campaign manager for American President Teddy Roosevelt.

Picture this scene: It is the year 1912. Teddy Roosevelt is nearing the climax of a hard fought presidential campaign. The final push is a whistle-stop tour through middle America.

At each stop Roosevelt plans to deliver an inspiring address and hand out thousands of pamphlets. On the cover of each pamphlet is an imposing presidential portrait; inside is a rousing speech. Hopefully, these will win over vital undecided voters.

The final tour is about to begin when a campaign worker notices a small printed notice on each photo: Moffett Studios—Chicago. The photograph is copyrighted and no one has obtained a clearance from Moffett.

Unauthorized use of the photo could cost a dollar for each pamphlet distributed. The prospect of a three million dollar bill sends a chill through the campaign workers. They simply can't afford it.

Yet the pamphlets are a crucial part of the re-election strategy. And if they go ahead without Moffett's permission and are caught, they will be branded law-breakers and be liable for a small fortune.

The campaign workers conclude they have no choice; they have to negotiate with Moffett, and there is no time to lose. You can imagine how they felt. Moffett seemingly has them over a barrel. Dejected, they seek campaign manager George Perkin's help. Perkins immediately instructs his typist to cable Moffett.

"We are planning to distribute many pamphlets with Roosevelt's picture on the cover. It will be great publicity for the studio whose photograph we use. How much will you pay us to use yours?"

The reply soon came back. *"We've never done this before, but under the circumstances, we'd be pleased to offer you $250."*

Legend has it Perkins accepted without asking for more.[134]

Frames don't only tell us what to pay attention to, they also tell us what to ignore. According to communications expert George Marshall, "frames are like a view finder of a camera and when we decide what to focus on, we are also deciding what to exclude."[135]

75 percent lean, 25 percent fat

To see how powerful framing can be, one group of people were told that ground beef was "75 percent lean", another was told the same product was "25 percent fat". Everyone was asked to guess how good it was.

The group that heard about "fat" estimated the meat would be 31percent lower in quality and taste—22 percent worse than the other group predicted. After both groups tasted burgers made from the same batch of meat, the "fat people" liked their burgers less than the "lean people" did.[136]

Framing a promotion

In 2004 two researchers, Joseph Nunes and Xavier Drize, set up a field experiment to test how the way promotions are framed influence the result of the promotion.

For months the researchers stood outside a carwash on Saturday mornings handing out two different types of loyalty cards. The first card urged customers to "buy eight carwashes and get your ninth wash free." Each time a customer came for a carwash their card was stamped.

The second promotion required customers to buy not eight, but ten carwashes before they got one free. The card also came with a special promotion: Customers were gifted two free stamps.

In absolute terms the two promotions were the same: Both required eight stamps before the customer could get a free car wash. The only difference between the two offers was the way they were framed.

The researchers found that 19 percent of the customers who received the first card (buy eight carwashes, get one free) completed the program. But an amazing 34 percent of customers who'd been given the second card with two free stamps completed the program—almost double that of those who received the first card.

Those who had been given the two free stamps were more likely to return and complete the program. They also took shorter breaks between visits. "Why did the framing make such a difference in customer decisions? The researchers concluded people expend greater effort towards achieving goals that they have already started than those they have yet to undertake."[137]

Brands act as frames

Compare the two well-known brands Starbucks and Wild Bean Café. Starbucks enjoys a significant price premium over Wild Bean Café. It is unlikely in a blind test consumers would be able to judge the difference between a Starbucks and Wild Bean Café coffee.

However, because Starbucks positions itself as a getaway, "a third place" between work and play, it is perceived to be more valuable than the momentary "pit stop" that Wild Bean Café offers. The extra profits the brand enjoys as a result of its "short holiday" framing are huge when you appreciate Starbucks sells over 2 billion cups of coffee each year.[138]

Single words can act as frames

In 1946 Churchill was a beaten man. The previous year he had lost the prime ministership after his conservative government had suffered an overwhelming election defeat.

Churchill wanted to warn the Western world about the spreading menace of Soviet communism. But he worried that the Americans wouldn't listen to someone who was now just the leader of an opposition party, rather than the head of an elected government.

Churchill's opportunity to convince Americans came when he was invited to speak in Fulton, Missouri. He knew he had to paint a vivid graphic of what was happening to countries like Poland and Czechoslovakia.

He toyed with words like "Soviet imperialism", "militarism" and "tyranny." But he rejected these as shapeless abstractions. None of these would paint a vivid enough picture in his listener's minds.

On the train down to Missouri, Churchill scanned his map of Europe. To highlight the spread of communism he drew a black pen line from the Baltic Sea through Poland down through to the Adriatic Sea. He retraced the line, searching his mind for the right image to describe the Soviet threat.

The inspiration came at 2.00 a.m. during an overnight stop in Salem, Illinois, when the right word picture appeared—which Churchill quickly added to his speech. The next day Churchill delivered the words that would mobilize the Americans into action: "From Stettin in the Baltic to Trieste in the Adriatic, an iron curtain has descended across the continent."

The iron curtain metaphor framed all subsequent debates about the Cold War. When China fell to Mao Zedong's Communists in 1949, the metaphor changed to bamboo curtain.[139]

The U.C. Berkeley linguist George Lakoff argues that the goal of good communication is to use "the words that trigger your frames and inhibit your opponents' frames."[140]

The iron curtain speech was, according to James C. Humes, author of *Churchill: Speaker of the Century*, Churchill's greatest speech. "Why was it the greatest? Because a single speech triggered a change in American feelings about the Soviet Union (American's wartime ally), and started the Americans to rearm."[141]

14.

Social Proof

Everyone Is Doing It

Following the crowd

In early 2009, Britain's tax collectors approached the consulting company Influence at Work, a company headed by three of the world's heavyweights from the world of persuasion science, Steve Martin, Naoh Goldstein and Robert Cialdini, with a multi-billion pound headache.

Over the years Britain's tax officials had tried a number of tactics to increase collection rates. Most threatened late payers with interest charges, late fees and legal action. While these tactics had some impact, the problem of late payers remained huge. Lots of British citizens weren't submitting their tax returns or paying what they owed on time.

Influence at Work recommended a different approach based on persuasion science. They asked the tax collectors to add a single sentence to their standard letter reminding the recipients of the large number of citizens who do pay their taxes on time.

The small "one sentence change" raised the tax collection rates in the targeted pilot study by a massive 29 percent. In total those letters, when combined with other techniques borrowed from the private collections industry, helped increase Britain's overdue tax collection revenue in a single year by £5.6 billion.

So why did so many people feel compelled to pay their taxes on time? The answer is social proof. Social scientists have known for years that "people's behavior is largely shaped by the behaviors of others around them, especially those with whom they strongly identify."[142]

Just as birds flock and bees swarm, humans follow the crowd.

Reducing energy consumption

A research team led by researcher and acclaimed expert on persuasion, Robert Cialdini, and chief scientist for OPOWER, a firm that advises utility companies how to reduce energy consumption, tested four different energy conservation messages on San Diego homeowners. They wanted to see what type of appeal would cause homeowners to conserve energy.

The first message urged homeowners to conserve energy for "the sake of the environment."

The second message urged homeowners to conserve energy for "the sake of future generations."

The third message urged homeowners to conserve energy "to save money."

The fourth message, using the power of social proof read, "The majority of your neighbors are undertaking energy saving actions everyday."

When the meters were read at the end of the month only one message made a difference.

Energy use only fell when households were informed that their neighbors were trying to do the same.

In a follow-up exercise run for OPOWER, Cialdini and his team sent residents a monthly letter that compared their own households' use of energy with the average energy use of their neighbors' and showed whether they performed worse, or better, than the average.

The homeowners who found they were worse at saving energy than their neighbors (and at cutting their power bills) quickly began to conserve more.

But there was a problem. Homeowners who discovered

they were doing better than their neighbors at conserving energy became more wasteful.

To solve the problem Cialdini cleverly added a smiley face next to their energy use figure. The smiley face had the effect of saying, "Well done; you are acting in accord with our community's shared values."

As a result, energy conservers continued their energy saving ways and energy use in the neighborhood went down.[143] Such is the power of social proof.

The bandwagon effect

People will often go with what they believe is the popular view. We laugh and clap at guests on television shows even when we know the initial clapping has been created electronically.

Opinion polls — Opinion polls tell us what other people are thinking and influence us on how to react. It's the power of social proof.

Saving souls — Arizona State University researchers secretly penetrated the Billy Graham organization. They found that before Graham ever arrived in town to preach, a local army of six thousand volunteers had been primed to "come forth at varying intervals to create the impression of a spontaneous mass outpouring."[144]

Telethons and social proof—If you've ever watched a telethon you may wonder why huge amounts of time and money are spent reading out the names of the people who have donated money. The message is: everyone else has given—so why shouldn't you?

Street buskers often place a few notes in their "tip boxes" to suggest to other donors that paper money is "standard." Similarly, church ushers salt their collection plates to guide their congregation in what is an appropriate offering.

Overcoming insecurity—Going with the crowd helps us overcome our insecurities. A multi-million-dollar investment in new computers seems much less risky if we know others like us have made the same choice.

When IBM totally dominated the computer industry, it was able to exploit these insecurities. Hence the expression: nobody ever got fired for buying an IBM!

Advertising and popularity—A prime purpose behind advertising is to increase a product's popularity. According to marketing professor Dr. Max Sutherland, "the more a brand is advertised the more popular and familiar it is perceived to be. Popularity is like a magnet. Advertising can enhance its power to attract. We as consumers somehow infer that something is popular simply because it is advertised."[145]

Advertising themes—Many advertisers tap into our need for social proof. Advertisers tell us their product is the number one brand, the largest selling or the fastest growing. Books are advertised as best-sellers. These advertisements don't push the product, they simply emphasize that everyone else is buying the product.

NOTES

1. Itamar Simonson and Emanual Rosen, *Absolute Value: What Really Influences Customers in the Age of (Nearly) Perfect Information*, HarperBusiness, 2014.
2. Ibid.
3. Kit Yarrow, *Decoding the New Consumer Mind: How and Why We Shop and Buy*, Jossey Bass, 2014, p. 19.
4. Ibid., p. 23.
5. Gary Small, *iBrain: Surviving the Technological Alteration of the Modern Mind*, William Morrow, 2008.
6. Exalcom Infographic 2016: What happens to an Internet minute.
7. Shlomo Bernatzi with Jonah Lenhrer "The Smarter Screen," *Portfolio*, 2015 pp. 12-13.
8. Daniel Bor, *The Ravenous Brain: How the Science of Consciousness Explains Our Insatiable Search for Meaning*, Basic Books, 2012.
9. Ibid.
10. Caitlin Dewey, "Six in ten of you will share this link without reading it a new depressing study says," *The Washington Post*, June 18, 2016.
11. Adrian J. Slywotzky with Karl Weber, *Demand, Creating What People Want Before They Know They Want It*, Headline e- book, 2011.
12. Ibid.
13. Chip Heath and Dan Heath, *Made to Stick*, Random House, 2007, p. 47.
14. Ibid.
15. Brian Fugere, Chelsea Hardaway and Jon Warshawsky, *Why Business People Speak Like Idiots*, Free Press, 2005, p.18.

16. Stephen Cone, *Powerlines: Words That Sell Brands, Grip Fans and Sometimes Change History*, Bloomberg, e-Book, 2008.
17. Ibid.
18. Ibid.
19. Ibid.
20. www.37signals.com.
21. Christopher Johnson, *Microstyle: The Art of Writing Little*, Norton, 2011, p. 9.
22. Ibid., p. 46.
23. Ibid., p. 46.
24. Ibid., p. 47.
25. Harry Mills, *Artful Persuasion: How to Command Attention, Change Minds and Influence People*, Amacom, 2000, pp. 111-112.
26. James Geary, *I Is an Other: The Secret Life of Metaphor and the Way It Shapes the Way We See the World*, Harper Collins, e-book, 2011.
27. Ibid.
28. Christopher Johnson, *Microstyle: The Art of Writing Little*, Norton, 2011, p. 92.
29. James Geary, *I Is an Other: The Secret Life of Metaphor and the Way It Shapes the Way We See the World*, Harper Collins, e-book, 2011.
30. Ibid., p. 95.
31. J. Scott Armstrong, *Persuasive Advertising: Evidence Based Principles*, Palgrave, Macmillan, 2010, p. 201.
32. Kit Yarrow, *Decoding the New Consumer Mind: How and Why We Buy*, Jossey-Bass, 2014, p. 33.
33. Oliver Payne, *Inspiring Sustainable Behaviour: 19 Ways to Ask For Change*, Routledge, e-book, 2012.
34. Steve Jobs introducing the iPhone at Macworld 2007, YouTube clip.
35. Bernadette Jiwa, *Make Your Idea Matter: Stand Out with a Better Story*, CreateSpace Independent Publishing Platform, 2012, p. 68.

36. Kevin Dutton, *Flipnosis: The Art of Split Second Persuasion*, Heinemann, 2010, p. 221.
37. John Caples, revised by Fred Hahn, *Tested Advertising Methods*, Fifth Edition, p. xviii.
38. Ibid.
39. J. Scott Armstrong, *Persuasive Advertising: Evidence Based Principles*, Palgrave, Macmillan, 2010, p. 30.
40. Ibid., p. 29.
41. Aaron Aders, "The Charm of 3 Approach to Marketing," *Inc.*, Dec 20, 2013.
42. Christopher Johnson, *Microstyle: The Art of Writing Little*, Norton, 2011, p. 44.
43. Ira Kalb, "Marketers Must Understand the Power of Three," *Business Insider*, May 5, 2013.
44. Sholomo Bernartzi with Jonah Lehrer, "The Smarter Screen," *Portfolio*, 2015, pp. 140-142.
45. Ibid., p. 143.
46. Ibid.
47. Ibid.
48. Ibid.
49. Matt Palmquist "We know who you are is a profitable pitch," *Strategy & Business*, April 14, 2016.
50. Folgers Coffee, Adsoftheworld.com.
51. Kit Yarrow, *Decoding the New Consumer Mind: How and Why We Buy*, Jossey-Bass, 2014, p. 172.
52. J. Scott Armstrong, *Persuasive Advertising: Evidence-Based Principles*, Palgrave, Macmillan, 2010, p. 119.
53. Burt Helan, "The Rise and Fall of David Ogilvy," *Business Week*, January 7, 2009.
54. J. Scott Armstrong, *Persuasive Advertising: Evidence-Based Principles*, Palgrave Macmillan, 2010, p. 111.
55. Marc Andrews, Dr. Matthijs van Leeuwen and Prof. Dr. Rick van Baaren, "Hidden Persuasion: 33 Psychological Influence Techniques in Advertising," *BIS*, 2013, pp. 36-37.
56. Harry Mills, *Artful Persuasion: How to Command Attention, Change Minds and Influence People*, Amacom, 2000, p. 193.

57. Ibid., p. 20.
58. Ibid.
59. Itamar Simson and Emanuel Rosen, *Absolute Value: What Really Influences Customers in the Age of (Nearly) Perfect Information*, Harper Business, 2013, p. 4.
60. Ibid., p. 4.
61. The Neilson Company, *Global Trust in Advertising and Brand Messages*, 2013 p. 2, p. 7.
62. J. Scott Armstrong, *Persuasive Advertising and Evidence-Based Principles*, Palgrave MacMillan, 2010, p. 124.
63. Harry Mills, *Artful Persuasion: How to Command Attention, Change Minds and Influence People*, Amacom, 2000, pp. 20-21.
64. Jack Ewing and Graham Bowley, "Even Before Diesel Scandal Bites, VW Loses Its Sales Crown," *The New York Times*, Oct. 26, 2015.
65. J. Scott Armstrong, *Persuasive Advertising and Evidence-Based Principles*, Palgrave MacMillan, 2010, p. 147.
66. Ibid., p. 148.
67. Quoted in Brian Sheehan, *Loveworks: How the World's Top Marketers Make Emotional Connections to Win in the Marketplace*, Powerhouse Books, 2013.
68. Chip Heath and Dan Heath, *Made to Stick*, Random House, 2007, pp. 195-199.
69. Adam Alter, *Drunk Tank Pink, and Other Unexpected Forces That Shape How We Think, Feel and Behave*, Penguin, 2013, p. 213.
70. James Geary, *I Is an Other: The Secret life of Metaphor and How It Shapes the Way We See the World*, Harper Collins e-books, 2011.
71. Ibid.
72. Jonah Berger, *Contagious: Why Things Catch On*, Simon & Schuster, 2013, p. 96.
73. Ibid., p. 106.
74. Ibid., p. 108.
75. Ibid., p. 109.

76. Ibid., pp. 111-112.
77. Ibid., pp. 103-104, p. 105.
78. Maria Konnikova, *The Confidence Game*, Cannongate, 2016.
79. Lisa Cron, *Wired for Story*, Ten Speed Press e-book, 2012.
80. Geoff Colvin, *Humans Are Underrated*, Portfolio, 2015, pp. 153-154.
81. Ibid.
82. Maria Konnikova, Ibid.
83. Adaptly, *Refinery29, Facebook, The Science of Social Media Advertising*, 20.
84. Amitav Chakravarti and Manoj Thomas, *Why People Don't Buy: The Go and Stop Signals*, Palgrave Macmillan, eBook, 2015.
85. Ibid.
86. Joseph Guinto, "Who Wrecked J.C. Penney," *D CEO*, Nov. 2013.
87. Amitav Chakravarti and Manoj Thomas, ibid.
88. Ibid.
89. Ibid.
90. Ibid.
91. Brian Christian. "The A/B Test: Inside the Technology That's Changing the Rules of Business," *Wired*, 04/25/12.
92. Ibid.
93. http://app.optimizely.com/signid
94. Ibid.
95. Shane Snow, *How Hackers, Innovators, Icons Accelerate Success*, Harper Collins. eBook. 2015.
96. Ibid.
97. Quoted by Matthew Willcox, *The Business of Choice: Marketing to Consumers' Instincts*, Pearson eBook, 2015.
98. Quoted in Eric Barker, *Barking Up the Wrong Tree*.
99. Quoted by Matthew Willcox, Ibid.
100. Ibid.
101. Ibid.
102. The Behavioral Insights Team EAST: "Four Simple Ways to Apply Behaviorial Insights."
103. Maria Konnikova, *Mastermind, How To Think Like Sherlock Holmes*, Cannongate 2013, p. 96.

104. Phil Barden, *Decoded The Science Why We Buy Wiley*, 2013.
105. Quoted by Matthew Willcox, ibid.
106. Noah Robischon, "BuzzFeed: For shaking up media across the globe," Fast Company, March 2016.
107. Ibid.
108. Ibid.
109. Ibid.
110. Ibid.
111. Sam Sommers, *Situations Matter: Understanding How Context Transforms Your World,* Riverhead Books, 2011, pp. 17-19.
112. Ibid., p. 50.
113. Ibid., pp. 51-52.
114. Thomas Gilovich and Lee Ross, "The Wisest One in the Room: How to Harness Psychology's Most Powerful Insights," *Oneworld*, 2016, p. 64.
115. Richard Nisbet, *Tools for Smart Thinking,* Allen Lane, 2015, p. 47.
116. Ibid., p. 46.
117. Natasha Dow Schull, *Addiction by Design: Machine Gambling in Las Vegas,* Princeton University Press, eBook, 2014.
118. Ibid. See also Matthew Crawford, *The World Beyond Your Head: How to Flourish in an Age of Distraction,* Farrar, Straus and Giroux eBook, 2016.
119. Ibid.
120. Ibid.
121. Ibid.
122. Ibid.
123. Ibid.
124. Ibid.
125. Ibid.
126. Douglas van Praet, *Unconscious Branding: How Neuroscience Can Empower (and Inspire) Marketing*, Palgrave Macmillan Trade, 2014.
127. Rolf Dobelli, *The Art of Thinking Clearly: Better Thinking, Better Decisions*, Sceptre, 2013, p. 26.

128. Gary Belsky and Thomas Gilovitch, *Why Smart People Make Big Money Mistakes: Lessons from the Life Changing Science of Behavioral Economics*, Simon and Schuster, 2010, p. 148.
129. Ibid.
130. Michael Shermer, *The Believing Brain from Ghosts and Gods to Policies and Conspiracies: How We Construct Beliefs and Reinforce Them as Truths,* Times Books, 2011, pp. 260-261.
131. Cass R. Sunstein, *How to Humble a Wingnut and Other Lessons from Behavioral Economics*, Chicago Shorts, 2014.
132. Philip Fernbach, "Extreme Political Attitudes May Stem From an Illusion of Understanding," *Association for Psychological Science*, April 29, 2013.
133. Quentin de la Bedoyere, *How to Get Your Own Way in Business, Gower*, 1990, p. xi.
134. Harry A. Mills, *Negotiate: The Art of Winning*, Gower, 1991.
135. George Marshall, *Don't Even Think About It: Why Our Brains Are Wired to Ignore Climate Change*, Bloomsbury, 2014, p. 80.
136. Jason Zweig, *You & Your Brain*, Simon & Schuster, 2007, p. 137.
137. Francesca Gino, Sidetracked: Why Our Decisions Get Derailed and How We Can Stick to the Plan, Harvard Business Press, 2013, pp. 178-179.
138. Phil Barden, *Decoded: The Science Behind Why We Buy*, Wiley, 2013, pp. 20-23.
139. George Lakoff and Mark Johnson, Metaphors We Live By, University of Chicago Press, 1980.
140. Ibid.
141. James C. Humes, Churchill: Speaker of the Century, Stern & Day, 1981.
142. Steve J. Martin, Noah J. Goldstein and Robert Cialdini, *The Small Big: Small Changes That Spark Big Influence*, Profile Books, 2014, p. 10.

143. Thomas Gilovich and Less Ross, *The Wisest One in the Room*, Oneworld, 2016, pp. 247-248.
144. Altheide and Johnson, "Counting Souls, A Study of Counseling at Evangelical Crusades," *Pacific Sociological Review* 20 (1977), pp. 323-348.
145. Max Sutherland, *Advertising and the Mind of the Consumer*, Allen & Unwin, 1993, p. 47.

ABOUT THE AUTHOR

Harry Mills is the founder and CEO of Aha! Advantage, an international consulting and training firm. For the past 27 years, the Aha! Advantage and its legacy firm, the Mills Group, have been helping a mix of global blue chip clients grow by improving their sales and message making.

Corporate clients include: GE Money, IBM, Ericsson, Oracle, BMW, AMP, Toyota, Lexus, Rio Tinto, Unilever, PWC, Deloitte, Ernst & Young and KPMG, ING and the ANZ Banking Group.

Harry Mills is the subject matter expert on persuasion for the *Harvard Business Review*'s flagship Manage/Mentor program, which goes out to 6.5 million managers.

He has built his reputation by translating the latest research of social psychologists, behavioral economists and neuroscientists into practical, cutting-edge insights and books.

Harry is the author of 14 acclaimed books on sales, presentation, persuasion and negotiation. They have been translated into 18 languages. His book *The Rainmaker's Toolkit, How to Find, Keep and Grow Profitable Clients* was selected by *CEO Advisor* as one of its top 10 U.S. business books in 2004 and described as the "new bible in professional services."

Harry is a regular keynote speaker at international conferences and is often interviewed on radio and television programs.